ARE WE LISTENING TO THE ANGELS?

ARE WE LISTENING TO THE ANGELS?

Edgar Cayce on Angels, Archangels and the Unseen Forces

By

Robert J. Grant

Are We Listening to the Angels? by Robert J. Grant
First Edition Published in 1994.
Second Edition (renamed Edgar Cayce on Angels, Archangels, and the Unseen Forces) Published in 2005.
Third Edition Copyright © 2019 by James M. Hart.

All rights reserved. No part of this publication may be reproduced, distributed, or transmitted in any form or by any means without the written permission of the publisher.

Images of Edgar Cayce used by permission–Edgar Cayce Foundation–Virginia Beach, VA; EdgarCayce.org

Prepared for publication by James Hart.
A Hart Warming Classics book.
www.HartWarmingClassics.com

ISBN-13: 978-4909069160
ISBN-10: 490906916X

Published in the United States.

*This book is dedicated
with love to my father and mother,
George H. and Mary Lou Grant*

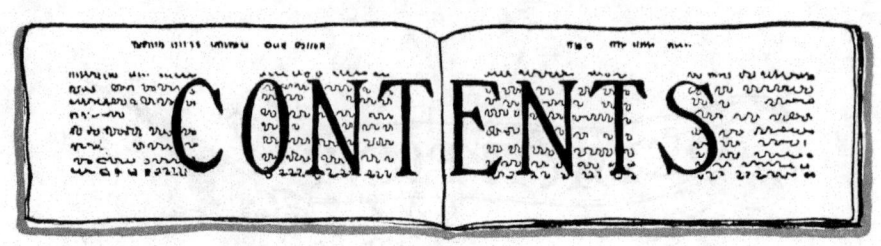

Chapter		Page
	Acknowledgments	vii
	Foreword	viii
	Preface	xii
1	We Are Not Alone	1
2	Chosen by an Angel	25
3	The Archangel Michael	45
4	The Lord of Karma	69
5	The Angelic Hierarchy	85
6	Satan and His Fallen Angels	105
7	The Angelic Promise - From Adam to Jesus	133
8	The Book of Revelation and the Angels Within	161
9	Our Beloved Guardian Angels	191
	About The Author	217
	Publisher's Note	218
	Bibliography	220
	Endnotes	223

Acknowledgments

Grateful acknowledgment is made to the following publishers for permission to reprint from their publications:

Return from Tomorrow, by George C. Ritchie, M.D., with Elizabeth Sherrill. Copyright © 1978 by George C. Ritchie, M.D. Reprinted by permission of Baker Book House Company.

The Boy Who Saw True, Anonymous, with Introduction, Afterword, and Notes by Cyril Scott. Copyright © 1953 by C.W. Daniel Company, Limited. Reprinted by permission of C.W. Daniel Company, Ltd., Publishers, 1 Church Path, Saffron Walden, Essex CB10 1JP, England.

Creating with the Angels - An Angels-Guided Journey into Creativity, by Terry Lynn Taylor. Copyright © 1993 by Terry Lynn Taylor. Reprinted by permission of H. J. Kramer, Inc., P.O. Box 1082, Tiburon, CA 94920.

Know Your Angels - The Angel Almanac with Biographies, by John E. Ronner. Copyright © 1993 by John E. Ronner. Reprinted by permission of Mamre Press, 107 Second Avenue, Murfreesboro, TN 37130.

All Scriptural quotations are from the King James Version of the English Bible. Quotations from *The Book of Enoch* are taken from the Richard Laurence translation; London: Kegan, Paul, Trench & Co., 1883.

The Association for Research and Enlightenment, Inc. (A.R.E.)., is an organization for those interested in the study and use of the Edgar Cayce psychic readings.

For reference purposes and to preserve anonymity, each person who received a reading from Cayce was given a number, which the reading carries in place of the name of the person. For example, reading 3902-2 was the second given for the person assigned the number 3902.

Foreword

IN the West we have come to depend on scientific evidence to support our theories about the world and the mysteries that still confound us. Given this hard-nosed empirical orientation, it is remarkable to me that so many people still believe in God today when God seems so unavailable to us. How is this faith sustained? When we scratch the surface of such faith, we usually discover that believers have surprisingly rich and varied experiential evidence of God's presence in their lives. Typically, they have had dreams, visions, and inexplicable happenings that form a personal foundation for their faith in the unseen.

Such experiences have not always been favorably considered by organized religion. Since the Reformation, Protestants in particular have looked suspiciously on anything, however sublime, that stands between an individual and his or her God. When the priestly hierarchy was swept aside by Martin Luther's effort to remove the then-perceived human barriers between ourselves and God, the spiritual hierarchy of angels and saints was deposed as well. Protestants were left trying to relate to God across a distance that was suddenly devoid of both human and divine mediators.

Not surprisingly, this condition could not last. For, whenever legitimate spiritual yearnings are suppressed - or thought to be unimportant or "unreal" - they eventually resurface in the private experiences of individuals everywhere. Today, in books like *Are We Listening to the Angels?* by Robert J. Grant, we see this happening in a dramatic way. Apparitions of Mary, encounters with Christ, and the manifestation of angels combine to form a compelling case that God reaches out to us across the barren divide.

I have written elsewhere about the modern-day encounters with Christ (*I Am with You Always*, published by Bantam Books in 1995). Consequently, I have often wondered about the relationship between angels and Christ, not so much from a theological standpoint, but from a psychological perspective - that is, from the standpoint of human need. I have asked, "Why do people *need* angels, and how does this need differ from their need for a more human Master or Redeemer?"

What occurs to me is that angels have always been the personal, albeit nonhuman, voice of God. They are, essentially, *emanations* from the highest reality that, nonetheless, stop short of becoming fully incarnate. Compared to human teachers and ministers, they remain forever pristine and unsullied by ordinary life. Angels give God a kind of rarefied dimensionality, like facets of a gem reflecting and revealing its intrinsic beauty. They are like colorful rays of the one Light, providing a particular hue to what is, in itself, all-encompassing and nonspecific. It occurs to me that we need this dimensionality in order to devise a plan for living. For, it is rarely satisfying enough to contemplate a nebulous wholeness when we are struggling with very definite issues down here.

Angels make a lot of sense psychologically because they bring the Divine closer to the human realm. But if angels have to do with God's *emanations*, then Christ has to do with God's *incarnation* - a step further in the process of God being expressed in personal form.

Drawing from several sources, Robert J. Grant makes a case that one angel in particular, the archangel Michael, was involved in helping to steward Christ's incarnation. Further, Michael seems to be active in our affairs as new developments are getting ready to unfold. One gets the sense that this angel oversees God's manifestations to the world. He is, one might say, the angel of *incarnation*.

Non-Christian readers may be interested to know that this relationship among God, angels, and the incarnation of God is depicted similarly in other religions. In Mahayana Buddhism, for instance, the universe is represented by the sacred mandala - a circular design which describes the relationship of the Divine to the phenomenal world. In the center of the mandala, the primordial Buddha, Vairocana, resides. Represented by white light, Vairocana is much like our transcendent deity who contains everything, but lacks specificity. Around him, however, are four *dyani* Buddhas who, like angels, have never been incarnate. Each of them expresses a particular attribute of the divine oneness, such as all-discerning wisdom or the wisdom of equality. One *dyani* Buddha, in particular Amoghasiddhi, represents all-accomplishing wisdom - the impulse to bring the Divine into material expression. Like Michael, this Buddha stands apart from the rest, somewhat, for he oversees the process of incarnation.

The importance of this angelic being to Mahayana is not surprising. For, in contrast to other forms of Buddhism, Mahayana Buddhism emphasizes that the highest achievement for any soul is to *return to earth* as an enlightened being - that is, to incarnate in order to enlighten the world. So it is not surprising that Mahayanists engage in the practice of moving Vairocana from the center of the mandala to the periphery and placing Amoghasiddhi in the center instead. By meditating on this new configuration, the meditator affirms the importance of incarnation over emancipation - a life of service even above the freedom that could be enjoyed by overcoming the cycle of rebirth.

Thus we can commune with angels, *dyani* Buddhas, and other archetypal beings who express God's dimensionality. And we can also commune with that angelic force whose impulse is to bring God down to live among us as a complete expression of the infinite in the finite.

In this inspiring and well-researched book, Robert J. Grant has done an excellent job describing angels from a variety of perspectives without overly concretizing these beings. By extending the range of angelic phenomena into areas not usually linked to angels per se, he reminds us that we are dealing most importantly with spiritual intervention that can assume a variety of forms. He thus leaves open the possibility that people perceive this intervention according to their own system of beliefs.

In one of the Christ encounters described in my book, *I Am with You Always*, a woman sees a Being of Light in the woods. She asks, "Who are you?" The Being says, "Some call me Buddha and some call me Christ." She then says, "I don't know Buddha." The Being replies, "Then I am Christ." This experience suggests that God does not have a problem with our need to experience Him according to our own beliefs and backgrounds: Spirit is delightfully and lovingly accommodating. And so, we should perhaps feel free to allow ourselves and others to relate to the Divine through the richly diverse, vital forms available to us. For a great many of us today, listening to the angels can be one of the best ways for us to enter into a life-changing communion with our deepest spiritual natures.

G. Scott Sparrow, Ed.D.

Preface

I have long been fascinated with the concept that there are angels who are able to guide, influence, direct, and inspire us in our lives from the unseen realms. I became convinced of the reality of angels during the time I spent as a hospice worker with the terminally ill. I witnessed many people who, free from pain in the last hours of their lives, became clear-minded and spoke of visions of angels who had come to help them to "the other side." Such experiences were not only a relief to the patient, but to the families who wished their terminally ill loved ones some respite from the ravages of cancer or AIDS.

According to many hospice volunteers I have spoken with, deathbed visions of angels are especially common among children. I do not believe that such visions are hallucinations from medication or intense pain. I do believe that just as we have a team of medical doctors and nurses who help in the delivery room with a baby being born into this world, I believe there are those spirits, angels, and guides who aid the dying - when a soul is "born" to the other side. I conducted an informal survey with friends and associates and found a surprisingly large number of people who believed they have had an encounter with an angel. These stories are what initially led me to conceive this book and examine the larger picture of the influence of angels in our lives.

Many books have been written about the reality of angels and their interaction with humanity. In this book, I have attempted to assert that the activities of angels in our time are not random at all, but that there is a purposefulness in their interaction that goes beyond individual transformation. There is currently a global shift or change taking place in our culture which, accompanied by the influence of angels, adds up to an exciting possibility: We are entering the dawn of an age of great spiritual awakening and fulfillment, and the angels are assisting us in this awakening.

Another interest, which led to my writing this book, is the fascinating life of the "sleeping prophet" Edgar Cayce, from whose work and psychic readings I have drawn extensively in this book. Cayce's life was drastically changed by the influence of angels. His actual encounter with one at age thirteen was the "tip of the iceberg" for him: He went on to become one of the world's foremost psychics, helping thousands of people during his lifetime with his unique and peculiar gift. After his encounter with the angel, Cayce was able to enter a self-induced sleep state and accurately answer any question posed to him. The accuracy of these answers has been well documented through his uncanny ability to diagnose illnesses and prescribe treatment for people he had neither met nor seen. Later in his life, people asked questions about the nature of angels and archangels and their role in humanity. These "answers" lend a fascinating view, not only of the archangels and guardian angels, but in the purpose of their manifestation in our time.

The information that Cayce gave while asleep are called "readings," of which there are more than 14,000. It can accurately be said that the encounter Cayce had with an angel was the first step in his role in the twentieth century as a modern-day prophet and seer. The angel directed him to a greater reality than he was previously aware of. I believe this is true with all angel experiences. The initial contact or experience is the *beginning*. I have written this book for the purpose of examining the larger picture of the angelic influence in relation to our personal and planetary spiritual evolvement: We are being directed to achieve a greater spiritual reality not by the angels alone, but by God who sends these angelic messengers to us.

It is true that humanity's interaction with angels has been occurring throughout the ages. However, there are critical times in the earth's evolution when the angelic presence is more influential. I believe this era is one such time. The information in Cayce's psychic readings indicate that we are now in the most important period in the world's history, a period where spirituality is being reawakened in the minds of people everywhere. As was true 2,000 years ago, the angels again are proclaiming this ascent in spiritual consciousness as they did during the time of Christ. My conviction in this belief is based on my more than fifteen years of research and study into Cayce's readings. Not only did Cayce give information on angels, he had *direct messages from angels* in his psychic readings which are applicable to each one of us even today. These inspiring messages are being given to us as preparation for a higher spiritual awareness which is just beginning to be born in our time. Yet it is our choice to either acknowledge and be a part of this growing spiritual consciousness or not to heed it and remain immersed in our material lives.

I was surprised that a book had not been written about Cayce's communion with angels. This material is important because his experiences confirm that we are not alone in our daily endeavors, and there is much more to be discovered when we examine their influence in relation to the spiritual evolvement of consciousness. This concept goes beyond an "angel phenomenon" and places the experience in the realm that humanity is changing, growing, and becoming more cognizant of the spiritual activity of the material world. It is my hope that this book will help the reader not only understand the angelic influences, but acknowledge that a spiritual call beckons each one of us in our own way.

In 1933, one young man came to Edgar Cayce to ask about psychic and angelic activity. He wanted to know what the highest psychic realization was. Cayce responded: "That God, the Father, speaks directly to the sons of men - even as He has promised."[1] I believe that the angels are the *direct voices* God uses to speak to us - if we would only listen. Other sources included in this book - Rudolf Steiner, George Ritchie, C. S. Lewis, Emanuel Swedenborg, *The Book of Enoch,* the Bible - as well as the Cayce readings, correlate this idea of angelic communication as a necessary step in our journey toward conscious communion with God.

People from all walks of life who have encountered angels are left with an incredible knowing which surpasses mere spiritual belief:

They know beyond a shadow of a doubt that God exists and is intimately aware and lovingly mindful of them. The angels, many believe, have been sent to remind us that in the midst of our sorrows and trials, there is always hope that we are loved and cared for by a Creator beyond our scope of comprehension. I personally believe that the angels are being sent to us by the Creator to enable us to realize that there is not a vast difference between the world of the seen and the Unseen. We are getting closer in consciousness to coming to a full, clearer understanding, not only of ourselves as souls, but of our relationship to God. This, I believe, is part of the greater message of the angels.

Chapter I

We Are Not Alone

"For he shall give his angels charge over thee, to keep thee in all thy ways. They shall bear thee up in their hands, lest thou dash thy foot against a stone." - Psalm 91:11-12

A Modern-Day Lazarus

DR. George Rodonaia, a Russian physician, psychiatrist, and scientist, was in a great deal of trouble. He had overstepped his bounds, but suspected nothing. As far as he knew, the Soviet Union was aware only of his work as a doctoral professor at Georgia University. But Dr. Rodonaia was wrong. The KGB had been tracking him as a political dissident and was aware of his secret activities with the underground. His primary job with the movement was to smuggle dissidents out of Russia to the United States and other democratic nations. They printed newsletters, networked with others of like mind, and were quickly mobilizing people toward a peaceful revolution. Communism was unacceptable to Dr. Rodonaia, and he was dedicated to the ideals of freedom.

The Kremlin knew that the esteemed professor was the enemy, and it had been planning his assassination in detail for many months. Ironically, Dr. Rodanaia felt himself to be in a safe place; he had managed to obtain an exit visa and had been invited to the United States due in large part to his scientific, medical, and scholarly university work.

He had achieved a reputable status in Russia as well. He held doctoral degrees in psychology, theology, science, and Oriental languages. He was in good spirits as he arrived at the airport in order to meet his family who were waiting to leave with him for the U.S. At last, he was leaving Russia behind to pursue a life unhindered by the limitations and oppression of communism. He didn't see the car idling less than a block away, nor did he see the watchful KGB as they followed his movements.

As the doctor stepped from the sidewalk to cross the four-lane avenue to the airport terminal, the KGB agent suddenly gunned his battered four-door and raced down the avenue toward him. The doctor only had time to see the oncoming car. He froze. The car hit him going forty-five miles per hour, throwing him into the road, fracturing his skull, and snapping his neck and spine. The KGB agents sped away from their assassination. Curious onlookers came into the street. By the time an ambulance arrived, Dr. Rodonaia was dead.

The medical technicians loaded his body into the ambulance and took it to the city morgue. An autopsy would be performed in several days. Ordinarily that would be the end of the story of Dr. Rodonaia, but after three days he would inexplicably awaken from death, only to reveal that he had had some extraordinary experiences in the worlds of the dead.

The soul of Dr. Rodonaia observed the removal of his body from the street at a curious vantage point: Above the scene, he saw the entirety of the last moments of his life and the placing of his body in a freezer.

Strangely detached, he turned his attention to his unusual surroundings. Darkness. Pitch. Black.

Where am I? he thought. *Am I not dead?* There was no anxiety. Floating in a sea of contentment, Dr. Rodonaia felt no pain, no anxiety.

A pinpoint of light began to appear in the darkness. Gradually the light grew, and he felt himself drawn to it. Moving closer to this light, he experienced immense joy and peace. Then, he was absorbed into the brilliance. He was alone, but felt utterly surrounded by an unfathomable love. He saw no one; no guides, no deceased relatives came to greet him.

He realized that the light was not a person, but an intelligence - alive - more alive than any person he had ever known. There were worlds within the light. Soon, he saw the light divided into sectors: other beings within a greater Being. He noticed that he, too, was a "light" like the sphere in which he found himself. He wanted to explore these radiating luminaries, and he immediately found himself immersed in spheres of light. They had names: Wisdom and Knowledge. Two distinct spheres of intelligence, but they had a common source.

Dr. Rodonaia marveled that the Knowledge and Wisdom he experienced were intelligences beyond his imaginings; they were the sources of everything which could be learned in the physical world. He would later reflect, upon awakening, that these celestial spheres were inclusive of the human spirit but greater - much greater than an earthly body or being. As he traveled within the infinity of this light, he experienced a form of universal knowledge. As quickly as he could mentally ask a question, an instantaneous answer presented itself. Dr. Rodonaia was amazed, because he was a scientist and never gave any thought to the continuation of the soul after death. A fuller joy than he had ever experienced on earth swept through him, carrying him to higher realms of understanding, harmony, and peace. Meanwhile, his body lay silent and forgotten in the morgue. Forgotten by his soul, as well as by his adversaries who had killed him.

Feeling more alive than he had ever felt on earth, Dr. Rodonaia drank in the brilliant understanding of life in all its aspects. He knew the ancient mysteries, the enigmas, the secrets of all ages. He absorbed the knowledge within the light, understanding that the universe is a thing alive, benevolent, omnipotent.

After what seemed like ages in this light, Dr. Rodonaia felt himself descending. Turning his attention to this descent, he saw the earth and the people he knew in his mortal life. He desired to know what was happening with his friends and family and found himself drawn into the home of his best friend, Maurice. The doctor continued to feel buoyant and serene - hovering high above the scene which unfolded itself like a play. Suddenly, his feelings of peace and harmony were replaced by dark thoughts. He watched his best friend staring helplessly into a crib which contained a small baby wailing in pain. Dr. Rodonaia, still in this unusual state of consciousness where every question could be answered by desire alone, understood what was happening instantaneously. Although his best friend did not know why the child had been relentlessly crying all day, Dr. Rodonaia knew immediately that the baby's hip was broken. A careless nurse had dropped the child and didn't report the accident. The parents came home to the screaming child, unaware of the tragedy.

Dr. Rodonaia wished that he could tell the little one to stop crying, that no one knew what the baby was trying to say. Even as this desire crossed the thoughts of his psyche, the child immediately stopped crying and looked up at Dr. Rodonaia. No one else in the room sensed the doctor's presence, but the child did. Dr. Rodonaia's friends were dumbstruck. The child had been crying all day! Why had it stopped?

He then felt himself being drawn upward, leaving this scene of his friend's and returning to the celestial fields of Wisdom and Knowledge. But the image he had just seen of the baby disconcerted him. He wished that he could do something to help. Upon the wings of this thought, he felt himself being drawn away from the light back into the darkness he had found himself immediately after his assassination.

The doctor had a great sense of anxiety as he felt himself leaving the light. Soon, he found himself again looking over another earthly scene: the hospital where his body had been taken.

The autopsy room! The pathologists had wheeled his cold and stiff body from the morgue onto the autopsy table. As the medical team began their posthumous work, cutting into his chest and abdominal cavity, Dr. Rodonaia began to lose his expanded consciousness, slipping further downward toward his body. Suddenly he felt cold. Freezing. Then he felt the heaviness of his body. The cold was unbearable. He tried to scream, but his vocal chords were frozen. He couldn't move any part of his body except his eyelids. He began to blink rapidly, hoping someone would see that he was conscious.

"It's alive!" the pathologist screamed. Pandemonium ensued. Medical trays and tools were knocked to the floor as the medical assistants jumped back in horror.

"Up to intensive care," one of the doctors screamed. "Immediately!" Dr. Rodonaia had begun to breathe again. He was wheeled into the emergency room, intravenous fluids were begun. A respirator was attached to help him breathe.

Dr. Rodonaia had come back from the dead after three days in the morgue!

"This is impossible," the pathologist muttered. "Impossible!"

When he regained full consciousness nearly a week later, Dr. Rodonaia saw his best friend standing at his bedside, wide-eyed and in shock.

"Your baby," Dr. Rodonaia croaked, speaking for the first time. "Your child's hip … it is broken … needs a doctor immediately … "

His friend looked on in astonishment. "George, George, how could you know what is wrong with my child?"

With as much urgency as he could muster, Dr. Rodonaia pleaded with his friend to take his child to the hospital. "The nurse dropped your child … injured … badly. Go! Now!"

The pain became intense, and Dr. Rodonaia fell unconscious. The man stopped at the nurse's station, telephoned his wife, and told her to bring the child to the hospital immediately for x-rays.

The child, near death at this point, was brought into the hospital. The x-rays showed the broken hip bone. A specialist was called in.

"The child will be well," the physician told the anxious parents.

Dr. Rodonaia's friend wept as he made his way to George's bedside. He grabbed his miracle friend's hand. "You saved my child … you saved my baby … "

His miraculous recovery was complete, with no brain damage. His spine and broken bones mended. Later, he successfully defected from the Soviet Union before the fall of communism and served as a pastor at St. Paul United Methodist Church in Baytown, Texas in the United States. He remembered in minute detail his three-day excursion into the world of the dead. As a result, he dedicated his life and work in service to humanity.

Dr. Rodonaia, who related this story during an interview in 1993, as well as in a short documentary film entitled *Life After Life*, never forgot his visit to the celestial worlds of Wisdom and Knowledge. According to an ancient text, *The Book of Enoch*, which was at one time part of the Bible, Wisdom is a divine intelligence - an angel - whose influence is learned in the schools of mysticism, while the actual source of wisdom remains in the realms unseen: "Wisdom went forth to dwell among the sons of men, but she obtained not an habitation. Wisdom returned to her place, and seated herself in the midst of the angels … " (*The Book of Enoch* 42:2)

Dr. Rodonaia felt that all of his scholarly education in life emanated from this realm, and during his three-day death occurrence he had the blessed experience of learning from the source of wisdom. In those three days, he felt that he learned more than he had in his thirty-six earthly years. He had never pondered the reality of angels prior to his death experience, and yet he knew after he awoke that it was they who guided him through many realms in the worlds unseen. This perspective of Wisdom and Knowledge as angels is quite different from the traditional view of divine messengers, and yet angels are defined as messengers who impart wisdom, inspiration, and guidance to human beings. Dr. Rodonaia's death experience is a powerful reminder to the living that there are worlds which have not yet been discovered, worlds in which the soul lives on.

He says that his time of death was "the greatest education of life anyone could hope for."[2]

An Angelic Rescue

Over the last century, there has been a dramatic increase in the number of people who have had miraculous experiences with angels. Anyone who studies the phenomenon will quickly conclude that there are unseen forces continually guiding and directing humanity's path. This seems paradoxical to the reasoning mind. To many, if something cannot be seen, it does not exist. People often scoff at the idea of invisible forces and psychic phenomena, but this thinking is being replaced by countless unexplainable encounters which indicate that something divine is indeed at work in the world today. The following story is a good example of one such otherwise unexplainable angelic encounter:

"Oh, my God, not now," Marie said aloud. "Please not now."

Marie Utterman's 1972 Dodge coughed and jerked on Interstate 95, outside of Richmond, Virginia. The car was losing speed as she pulled onto the shoulder. It died a quiet death, no smoke, no steam, no loud crunching of the engine. But Marie knew it was indeed dead, nonetheless. The transmission had been on its way out for months now.

She had been en route to Washington, D. C., from Norfolk, Virginia. Her daughter was due to have her baby in a few short weeks, and the pregnancy had been a difficult one. Marie had felt a sense of urgency about her daughter all morning long. She couldn't shake the sense of unease when she thought of her. Her preoccupation became an anxiety which would not leave her alone.

Go to her. Go to Jenny. Hurry.

Finally, she followed her intuition after calling Jenny's telephone and receiving the answering machine. *Jenny should have picked up the phone*, Marie thought. *She's always home at this hour.*

"Jenny, it's Mom," Marie said after the machine's beep. "Honey, I'm coming to D. C. I know you'll say I don't have to, but I'm coming. I hope you're all right. See you soon."

She's going to think I'm crazy, Marie thought. She wasn't one to meddle in her daughter's affairs, but this *feeling* demanded that she go to her right away. "Mother's intuition," she muttered as she packed a small suitcase. "God, I hope I *am* crazy."

Marie rested her head on the steering wheel, reliving the early morning events which had delivered her to this helpless roadside dilemma. She was several miles east or west from the nearest exit. She was also two hours away from her daughter's home outside Alexandria, Virginia.

"God, please help me," Marie said. "I've got to get to Jenny. *Please*."

Marie knew nothing about automobiles, but decided she'd pop the hood anyway. "Maybe it's a wire. Maybe it's just a damn wire that's loose."

Cars zoomed past as she stepped out of the Dodge. It was nearing rush hour on Interstate 95; she doubted anyone would think to stop. She lifted the hood and propped it open. No loose wires. Just a dead engine. She climbed back into the Dodge after shutting the hood. Eyes closed, with all the hope she could muster, she turned the key, visualizing the car roaring into life. The engine turned, but did not catch. Marie felt completely helpless. Tears sprang into her eyes as she looked at the busy interstate. "Please," she whispered to the cars speeding by. "Oh, please … I've got to get to Jenny!"

As her plea fell from her lips, a nondescript white van pulled onto the shoulder in front of Marie. The driver had turned on his emergency flashers and was reversing the van to back up to Marie's car.

Marie was incredulous, but enormously relieved. "Oh, oh, thank God," she said.

We Are Not Alone

The driver's, passenger's, and large side doors of the van opened at once, and three what appeared to be college-age men stepped out. They looked about twenty-four or twenty-five years old, the same age as Jenny. Marie felt immediately at ease upon seeing the young men. They were very handsome, clean cut, and smiling. She thought they must have been on their way to a club meeting, as they were all dressed in white polo shirts, white windbreakers, and loose-fitting white slacks. *Maybe they're interns at the hospital*, Marie thought as she rolled her window down.

The blond man smiled reassuringly at Marie. "Ma'am, if you'll step out of the car, we'll see if we can get it going again." Marie didn't hesitate.

"I can't begin to thank you," she said, stepping out of the car. "I've got to get to my daughter. She's going to have a baby, and … "

Marie told her story as the three men pulled tool-box and hydraulic jack from the back of the van. The car jack was shining and new. They smiled at Marie and nodded as she explained her dilemma. They didn't hesitate in beginning their work.

Seeing that they intended to fix the car right there, Marie began to protest. "You boys are all dressed for some sort of outing. Please, if you just get me to a phone I'll have one of my daughter's friends meet me or I'll have her husband come and help. You don't have to … "

"No problem, ma'am," the blond man said as he crawled under Marie's car. "We'll have you back on the road in a minute."

"Hand me that socket, Mitch." Marie noticed that Mitch resembled her son-in-law, Jenny's husband. He excused himself and stepped around Marie, digging into the tool set.

"O. K.," said the blond to the other man, "now hand me the needle-nosed pliers."

For the next five minutes the blond man asked for tools like a surgeon asks for instruments during surgery. Mitch crawled under the right side of the car and helped his friend. The third gentleman was reaching into the engine beneath the opened hood.

Why, they'll get grease all over their clothes, Marie thought. She had never felt so grateful in all her life. She noticed that her anxiety had completely subsided. She felt quite content - actually buoyant. Strange, under the stressful circumstances, that she should feel so calm. The three men spent a total of ten minutes working on Marie's car. Mitch climbed out from under the car and slid in the driver's seat. He turned the key. The Dodge coughed, then started, idling perfectly. Marie was astounded. As quickly as Mitch started the auto, he got out of the car and walked over to her. "I think it's going to be O. K.," he said. "You're back in business."

Marie was overwhelmed with gratitude. "I can't tell you how grateful I am. Please, I want to pay you for your trouble." She reached into her wallet and began to give them the spare fifty-dollar bill she kept stashed for emergencies.

The three young men began to load their tools and jack into the back of the van, ignoring Marie's outstretched hand. Mitch paused after putting the jack into the van and smiled at her. "That won't be necessary," he said. "This is what we're here for." The three exchanged a mutual acknowledgment to one another, nodding. Marie was momentarily taken aback - not because they wouldn't take the money, but because of their appearance. For the first time, she noticed that the young men did not have a bit of dirt or grease on their clothing, nor on their hands. Their white apparel was as clean as when they stepped from the van.

Marie found herself feeling as if she were in a dream. "How could you ... I mean ... you've been crawling around on the ground ... you should be - "

"You need to get going, ma'am," the brunette man said. "Your daughter needs you."

The reminder brought Marie out of her astonishment. "Oh, yes! I'll be on my way then. But how can I thank you?" She started toward the three men, feeling so drawn to them, almost as if she knew them from somewhere.

"You already have," the blond man said with a casual salute. "You take care now."

Stepping back, Marie had to hold onto the front fender of her idling car for support. She felt a bit unsteady. *Were they sent to help me?* she thought. For the first time in her life, she believed in angels. There was no other way to explain what had just happened. She knew from what her mechanic neighbor had said that when the transmission decided to die, it would be dead until it was replaced.

Marie watched in a state of awe as the van climbed the hill on Interstate 95 East. Before it topped the horizon, it vanished. Although she was quite unsettled, she hurried back onto the interstate to her daughter's home in Alexandria. She had only lost a total of fifteen minutes in her travel time.

When she arrived, Marie parked in Jenny's driveway and quickly banged on the front door. No answer. She checked the door and found it unlocked.

"Jenny! *Jenny!*" Marie called out as she walked into the house. "It's Mom! Where are - ?"

Marie stopped suddenly, staring at the figure on the kitchen floor. Jenny was lying there, blood pooling around her lower abdomen and hips. She quickly knelt by her daughter, checking her breathing and pulse. Her color was ashen, but she was breathing. Marie quickly dialed 911. Even in the midst of her panic, a vision of the three men along the interstate filled her thoughts. She quietly, calmly gave the emergency operator her daughter's address and explained the scenario. Marie felt partly detached, like an observer of the scene. *My daughter will live*, the detached part of her said. *She will live.* In her vivid memory the three men smiled at her.

Marie listened closely as the operator gave her instructions for Jenny. She hung up the telephone, checked Jenny's hemorrhaging which appeared worse than it actually was. She fetched a blanket from the living-room couch and draped it over her daughter, placing a pillow under her head. Part of Marie couldn't believe that she felt so calm, so reassured.

The emergency team arrived, burst through the front door, and knelt beside Marie's unconscious daughter. Jenny's blood pressure was dangerously low. They started intravenous fluids, as they conveyed her into the ambulance.

One of the EMTs told Marie that Jenny was going to survive. "Her pressure is low, but it's not dropping. Her pulse is steady. Thank God you got to her in time."

"Yes, thank God," Marie agreed. Because there was room only for Jenny and the EMTs, Marie followed the ambulance in her car to the hospital, which was only fifteen minutes away. The image of the three men in her mind kept her calm and certain.

"You need to get going, ma'am. Your daughter needs you." The echoes of their voices comforted her.

Jenny's baby was delivered via an emergency Caesarean section. She was given transfusions and she stabilized. Marie's grandson, Michael, was delivered three weeks premature. The attending physicians were amazed that the mother and child recuperated so quickly. Jenny and the baby went home within a month.

Marie told very few people of her unusual happening on the interstate. She was a down-to-earth, pragmatic type of person. Nevertheless, the experience opened her to a whole new perception of life. After Jenny delivered her baby, Marie had a series of dreams in which she saw the young men who helped her. In the dreams, they were enveloped in a white light. They were standing on what appeared to be a large white balcony of a theater. Marie was on stage below them. After pondering the dreams for some weeks, she came to the conclusion that they were trying to send the message to her that she was never really alone, that there was always someone watching over her. She interpreted the stage in her dream to be "life's stage where dramas are played out." The angels in the balcony she knew were watching and taking care of her. After what she had been through with her daughter, Marie not only believed in guardian angels, she knew them to be a fact of life.

Reassuring Angels

At times, we receive miraculous reassurances not only from loved ones, but from unseen beings who comfort us, the living, during times of grief. The following story illustrates that there are divine presences with us in our darkest hours:

Darrell Cook was grief-stricken. His mother had died suddenly at age sixty. The young man had known that his mother's diabetes was taking its toll upon her health, but had been reassured by family members that her brief hospital stay was only for tests and minor treatment for her elevated blood sugar.

He was standing outside his childhood home in Indiana, admiring his mother's beloved garden, reliving the phone conversation he'd received the day before:

"Darrell, this is Diane," his sister had said. "Mom died today at 2:30 p. m. Dad went in to see her in the hospital and she was just gone ... "

Numbness was the only thing he felt on the trip from Florida to Indiana to attend his mother's funeral. The trip was a blur. *She just can't be gone*, he thought. *Dad said she was doing all right.*

Death was a mysterious stranger to Darrell. He'd never before lost anyone he had loved. He looked out at the flower garden his mother had tended for more than thirty years, and he wondered who would tend the garden now.

Darrell's mother's death was all the more difficult because the two had never been particularly close, but one thing they shared was the beauty of nature. Her gardens used to be a comforting place to be. Now, however, the sight of the garden and birds brought Darrell nothing but pain. There had been no closure with his mother - no final words, no good-by. He had come to the garden to say his goodbyes, but he found he wasn't able to say his farewells here. It was too ... alive.

He climbed into the family's 1969 Mustang convertible and drove to the small cemetery where his mother had been buried weeks before. *Mom, maybe I can say good-by to you there*, he thought, as he drove the short distance to the cemetery. The sunset was particularly spectacular. He abruptly stopped in front of her tombstone. What he was seeing couldn't possibly be real.

A robin, his mother's favorite bird, had built a nest atop the flower centerpiece on the gravestone and was watchfully sitting upon the nest. As his amazement grew, Darrell noticed that the mother bird was nesting on four eggs. He was awestruck. *Why would the mother robin build her nest here and not in the secluded trees surrounding the grave?*

"Mom ... " Darrell said aloud. "Oh, Mom ... " He sat for a long while and gazed upon this strange event. He knew then that he could go back home to his mother's beloved garden and say good-by; the experience would not be painful. Darrell's feelings of grief left him as if they had been a physical thing. He was, inexplicably, completely at peace now.

As he drove back to his home, Darrell found himself speaking aloud to his mother, saying all the things he wanted to express had she been alive. He felt flooded with relief. He parked the car in the driveway and walked the short distance to his mother's garden in the back yard. He could feel her presence physically now. She was unseen, but felt very near.

Beside the archway of vining pink roses, Darrell noticed a group of plants he had never seen before. A cluster of peony-like flowers, whose centers resembled those of roses, sat next to the archway. The colors of the flowers were more brilliant than the others; they were burgundy, with maroon petals and a yellow pistil in the center of each.

What kind of flowers are those? Mom never had flowers like that. The flowers were fully open, like a morning glory, but the petal configuration looked like peonies.

Darrell brought his father out to the garden to look at this unusual phenomenon. "No," his dad said, "she would never plant anything in that area of the garden - not next to the roses." He, too, was bewildered. "I've looked at this garden for thirty-five years and have never seen such a thing." The peculiar flowers even behaved like morning glories: For the next three days, they opened in the morning and closed at night. Then they died, leaving behind their bright green foliage. Darrell and his father took the appearance of the flowers as a sign. A special message from beyond the grave.

"Do you believe in angels, Dad?" Darrell asked.

"I do now," he replied.

It is difficult to say whether Darrell's experience was from his mother or from an angel. Either way, a miraculous reassurance was given to him and his family which transformed their views of death and dying. Darrell knew, after this experience, that his mother *lived on*.

An Angel Visits a Dying Man

Doreen had been distraught for weeks. Her husband's cancer was not going into remission. The chemotherapy had not even slowed its progress. Before her eyes, David was slowly withering away. He was having difficulty walking. The cancer had spread from his liver to his spine and was now affecting his limbs. His fevers were raging the night Doreen checked him into the hospital.

She stayed with him until he fell into a drug-induced sleep. He had been in terrible pain recently, it was getting worse, and he was beginning to rely more and more upon the morphine for relief.

When Doreen came to visit David the following day at the hospital, he wasn't in his room. She inquired at the nurse's station and was told that the last time anyone had checked on him, he was in his room.

"You don't understand," Doreen said, "he's having trouble *walking*. Someone had to help him out of bed."

A couple of nurses went with Doreen to look for David. He was not in the lounge, nor was he in the bathroom. Finally, Doreen walked to the end of the hall and opened the door to the chapel. She found David sitting there with a teen-aged boy with blond hair.

"David, I've been looking all over for you," Doreen said, a little dismayed. "What are you - "

"I'm fine," David replied, not looking at his wife. "I'll be out in a few moments."

Doreen wondered who David was talking to. Suddenly, the boy turned and looked at her. She instantly was filled with a sense of calm and peace.

"The boy had the most other-worldly eyes," Doreen said later. "I've never seen eyes like that on anyone. When he turned his eyes to me, I felt this wonderful, buoyant calmness. I knew that David was all right and that he needed this time to be with this boy. I knew to leave immediately."

Doreen left David in the chapel and waited. After thirty minutes, David emerged and was walking with ease. Doreen tried to hide her surprise. Yet when she looked at him, she knew that he had had some extraordinary experience. A light seemed to emanate from him and surround him like an aura.

"David, who was that?" she asked.

"You wouldn't believe me," he replied.

"Try me."

"That was my guardian angel." Doreen, who had never even discussed such things with her husband, instantly believed. Her husband, who the day before had been sickly and pale, looked exuberant, out of pain, and at peace. She quickly ran down the hall to the chapel to get another glimpse of the boy she saw with her husband.

"He's not in there," David called after her, almost laughing. "But if it will make you feel better to go check, please be my guest."

Doreen found the chapel empty and looked in amazement at her husband.

"What did he say to you, David?" she asked quietly.

David proceeded to tell his wife that his guardian angel asked if there were any deeds for which he would like to be forgiven. He listed some unresolved conflicts and incidents, and the angel said that those things were forgiven. The angel then reassured David and said that everything was all right.

The most dramatic aspect of this story is its aftermath. After David's encounter with the angel, he became a comforter to many people in the hospital. He did not spend much time in his own room, but roamed the hospital visiting patients and talking with them. Doreen reports that her husband in his latter days had no fear of death. He had been afraid of death, however, prior to the visit with the angel.

Doreen mistakenly thought that David's encounter with the angel meant that he would survive the cancer. He did not. Within two weeks of his angelic encounter, David painlessly left this world.

"He was at great peace in the end," Doreen said. "He was even excited at the prospect of his new life out of his cancer-ridden body. He did not survive physically, but I know that he was healed spiritually. I know the angel came to comfort him in his last days." The aftermath of David's passing was easy for Doreen. She had anticipated a long period of grief and loneliness. There was none. She felt the presence of her husband and his guardian angel.

"I was at peace," Doreen said. "I knew it was David's time to return home. And I know that it was an angel who helped David and then helped me over my grief."

The Reassurance of Angels Among Us

The above stories confirm that angels are sent by God to assist and reassure us in times of personal crisis. In each case, there was a critical need and an intervention beyond the explanations of the physical world that came to those needing help. Dr. Rodonaia's case is all the more fascinating because of his miraculous return from death after three days. The message here is that we may be in the seemingly limited, physical world, and yet we still have a connection to the spiritual realms through which miracles can happen. This confirms what Jesus said to His persecutors prior to the crucifixion: "Thinkest thou that I cannot now pray to my Father, and he shall presently give me more than twelve legions of angels?" (Matthew 26:53) It has been said that Jesus came to show humanity what was possible by attuning to the spiritual realms. If Jesus promised that we would do all the things He could do, then it stands to reason that we all have the power to summon the angels in time of need. More and more documented occurrences of angelic activity happening world-wide bring home the idea that there is so much more to us, in the spiritual sense, than we have been previously aware of.

In recent years many books, articles, movies, and television shows have been exploring the paranormal phenomenon of seen and unseen guardians or guides leading everyday people to physical safety, emotional peace, or inner transformation. While the four accounts above are diverse and seem to be unrelated, there is a common thread that connects each story: When it seems that we are beset by depthless grief, when there are occasions where it appears that disaster or death is imminent, intervention can occur which inexplicably averts the disaster, the death, and brings healing, peace, and a knowledge that the angels are aware of us.

These experiences don't fit in what traditionally have been called angelic encounters; there were no winged beings descending from the heavens to deliver people from trouble. Yet, if we examine the idea that angelic experiences are attributed to the divine Source, then we may conclude that this Source has infinite ways of manifesting in a material world. Since ancient times, angels and archangels have made appearances to humans who were in dire circumstances or who were in the depths of despair and needed comfort or a restoration of faith. Angelic encounters have inspired visions, prophetic dreams, and miraculous healings. Often there is a physical manifestation such as that Marie experienced when her daughter was in trouble or David who spoke with his guardian angel.

The sacred texts of most religions teach us that the generations that went before us not only received the intervention of benevolent forces, such as angels and archangels, but actually relied on these forces for directing the activities in their lives. Throughout the Scriptures, angels came to men and women in dreams and in waking consciousness. Inspired by them, prophets spoke of coming events proclaimed by them, and the events were often heeded by the people of that day. The chosen people were continually reminded that there is a divine order. This belief was held not merely among small independent groups but among the masses.

Our present time is a reaffirmation that the Divine is just as cognizant of us as in those ancient biblical days. As Jesus raised Lazarus from the dead 2,000 years ago, Dr. George Rodonaia came back to life after being dead three days in the 1970s. A mother, deeply concerned for her daughter's welfare, was helped by a mysterious group of men who vanished after fixing her car. A terminally ill man, after encountering an angel in a chapel, was reassured and given strength in order to face his death. A young bereaved man was given the spiritual reassurance at his mother's grave and in her garden that she was not really dead at all. These present-day wonders of angelic intervention represent only a few of the thousands which are being recounted throughout the world.

On December 27, 1993, *Time* magazine reported that sixty-nine percent of America's population believe in angels. In the cover story, correspondent Nancy Gibbs wrote: "What idea is more beguiling than the notion of lightsome spirits, free of time and space and human weakness, hovering between us and all harm? To believe in angels is to allow the universe to be at once mysterious and benign. Even people who refuse to believe in them may long to be proved wrong."[3]

Many people believe that the intervention of unseen, benevolent forces is not a phenomenon at all; it is - as the word "angel" translates - a "divine message" or call to humanity from God. A call to what? In the historical perspective, angelic beings and forces call upon humans to acknowledge, dedicate, and remember that there are spiritual matters at hand which are of critical importance.

We are inclined to believe that the experiences reported in this chapter are rare and exceptional. However, the thousands of angelic encounters being reported by everyday people leads one to the conclusion that humanity as a whole is being called to a special mission, a special role in this peculiar spiritual renaissance. On the whole, the angelic manifestations in people's lives are as diverse as the people themselves. Spontaneous healings are taking place, faith is restored, people are returning from clinical death with no brain damage after being dead three days. Imminent, potentially fatal car accidents are miraculously averted.

A common theme runs through the many angelic experiences being reported: *We are not alone, nor have we ever been.* Help is close at hand. It is interesting to note that the people whose stories are related in this chapter did not consider themselves devoutly religious. They didn't necessarily believe in angels. Rodonaia was a Russian philosopher who gave little thought to a "God." Because of his training and education in the Soviet Union, he believed only in the mind. Marie hadn't been to a church since she was a teenager. Doreen and her husband were preoccupied with the medical complications of David's illness and didn't take the time for spiritual communion. Darrell had an antagonistic view of the church because of fundamentalist teachings as a child, teachings which had never been explained to him. He had not visited a church since he was a teenager.

We Are Not Alone

What these people did have, however, was a crisis. In Dr. Rodonaia's case, his crisis was physical: The KGB attempted to murder him. In Marie's case, her crisis was emotional *and* physical: Her daughter was in grave danger. In Darrell's case, his crisis was spiritual: He questioned the fundamental puzzles and anxieties about life and death, and had suddenly lost his mother without any closure. In these cases, a definite reassurance was present to say, *you are not alone.* In each case, like the thousands who report angelic and miraculous experiences, their lives and attitudes were transformed.

Help for the World

A new awakening is coming to humanity via people who have had miraculous or angelic encounters. Although these paranormal happenings with divine beings may seem like something new, they are only reminding us or reacquainting us with the idea that we have always had access to a spiritual form of aid and intervention. The angelic beings have, since the beginning of our creation, manifested and guided us back to the first premise: *You are not alone - God is mindful of you.* But it is up to us to take hold of that idea and invite a divinely guided life.

It may be difficult to believe that the angels can actually represent a great hope to us in the midst of a world in crisis. Indeed, the world's appearance can be deceiving: We see the devastation of countries at war. Plagues and famine are rampant across the globe. Earthquakes and floods are happening at an unprecedented rate. Economic instability is the mainstay of our times. Crime is at an all-time high in the United States. These conditions are not new, for they were even present during Christ's time. Jesus came in the *midst* of such crises. What he proclaimed was a hope beyond what the world had previously known: "For the Father loveth the Son, and sheweth him all things that himself doeth: and he will shew him greater works than these, that ye may marvel." (John 5:20) Christ taught the importance of the inner spiritual life; He taught that the kingdom of heaven is *within* the soul and spirit. His teachings also reflect that we are cared for by a loving God who is cognizant of our struggles as well as our hopes. In the midst of this, however, Jesus taught that the world of appearances was falling apart and would continue to fall apart as long as humanity ignored the inherent spiritual essence behind the material world.

That the world is being shaken up in unparalleled ways is itself a divine call that seems to say: *Remember where you came from - you are a spiritual being first.* If the material world were not undergoing massive change and upheaval, would humanity have any reason to seek out a spiritual world? Would we not be a world self-satisfied and content? If the thousands of angelic encounters are true, it stands to reason that the Creative Forces, or God, are actively pursuing us, to "wake us up" and remember our divine heritage. The angelic encounters are, in many ways, telling us that we are fast approaching a new spiritual consciousness; a conscious, aware spirituality unknown in recorded history. This philosophy is at the heart of what the prophets and sages have said throughout the ages: The day will arrive when humanity will have a conscious relationship with the Creator, with God. The potential for a wonderful ascent to a higher spiritual consciousness is upon us. It is indeed amazing that the angels are calling.

What is more amazing still are the possibilities that await our planet when we begin to listen to that call. And how shall we begin to listen? Let's take a look at someone else who not only *heard* angels but *saw* them, too.

We Are Not Alone

Chapter 2

The Sleeping Prophet

"And these signs shall follow them that believe; In my name ... they shall speak with new tongues ... they shall lay hands on the sick, and they shall recover." - Mark 16:17-18

Chosen by an Angel

THERE is no greater source of information on angels than an impressive body of knowledge that came into being in a most unconventional way.

During the first half of this century, a remarkable man, Edgar Cayce, used his unique psychic ability for the purpose of helping those who came to him for advice. He became known as "the sleeping prophet" and "the man who could see through time and space." When someone would go to him for help, Edgar Cayce would lie down, meditate and pray, and enter a sleeping, trance-like state. During the  time he was unconscious, recipients would receive extremely accurate information from a source beyond the awareness of the sleeping Cayce. They would receive information of which Cayce had no knowledge during his waking state.

The story of this amazing man's psychic ability and his own extraordinary experiences with angels is an important step in understanding the meaning of angelic experiences in our lives and in the overall evolution of humankind.

A Stranger to the Earth

If the uneducated young Cayce had had the vocabulary to describe himself, he would have said, "I am a stranger to the earth." Even when he wanted to fit in with his friends and family, he often felt a world apart. In 1888, during his early childhood, Edgar was able to (as he put it) "see things." Sometimes he felt he was actually seeing what people thought. Cayce, who would grow up to be the world's best-documented psychic, was not necessarily reading people's minds. He was reading a life-energy pattern which vibrates all around our physical bodies in different shades and colors. The mystics in the East would call these colors the life essence or aura. Edgar had observed these auras all his life, and he knew that when he saw a red color pattern around people, they were angry. If he saw gray or black hues surrounding someone, he could see that that person carried grudges and resentment. If Edgar looked long enough at these colors, he could see the actual thoughts of the people. To him, it was like reading books.

As a child, Edgar thought everybody saw these color patterns of people's thoughts and feelings. His classmates made sport of him when he would talk about the bright or dark colors surrounding his friends.

"You're a crazy old man," they would say, laughing. "Old Man" was a name given to him by his grandfather. Perhaps it was because, to those who could sense it, Edgar seemed wise, an "old soul."

He finally talked with his mother about the peculiar things he saw. His mother always knew that her son was special.

"It's a gift, son," she said. "Don't you mind what people say about it. Just don't try to see too much; it'll upset you."

Edgar knew his mother was right. Sometimes grown-ups would think things that didn't make much sense; many grown-up conversations he couldn't understand either. He saw the color patterns, shades, and adult thoughts and was more than a little confused. So he tried to see and understand only the brighter side of people's thoughts. His mother encouraged Edgar to read the Bible so that he might find the answers about his abilities there.

"God has a special plan for you, Edgar," his mother told him. "You just pray about it."

Edgar always felt better after he talked with his mother. She didn't laugh at him or call him crazy when he told her of his visions. A lot of people said that Edgar had imaginary playmates. But Edgar's mother could see the "elementals," too. She called them Edgar's "nature playmates." On the days when Edgar would be feeling rather low or quiet, his mother would glance out the window and see the nature spirits waiting for him. "Your playmates are here," she would say. Edgar would run outside to meet them. Funny, they looked just like little boys and girls. He wondered why no one else but he and his mother could see them. Years later, Edgar would read books and articles about the fairies and gnomes, the guardians of the plant and animal kingdoms. He would listen in a mild state of amusement while his friends hotly debated whether these elemental beings were real or not. Edgar didn't debate. These elementals had been his friends throughout childhood.

As a child, Edgar learned to keep his comments about his secret friends quiet - except to tell his mother. She would tell him stories about his grandfather, Thomas Jefferson Cayce, who also had visions and psychic experiences.

"He had the second sight," his mother said. "Best dowser in Christian County. Wherever he'd point that stick of his, why they'd find water." Edgar loved his grandfather and was heartbroken when he was killed in a bizarre accident in rural Kentucky. He cried to his mother and wanted to know why his grandpa had died. Edgar's mother explained that it was time for Grandpa Cayce to go back to heaven and be with the angels. Edgar saw little use for Grandpa being up with the angels when he was needed down here on earth. He shared his grief with the family's servant Patsy, who reassured him that he would see his grandpa again. "You got the second sight, Edgar." It wasn't the last time young Edgar Cayce would hear those words. Right then, though, it didn't seem to make a bit of difference *what* kind of sight he had; he just missed his grandfather.

Cayce didn't think much about what people called his "second sight" until one day when he was in the barn and saw an apparition of Grandpa Cayce. The sight of him didn't startle Edgar, as he looked just like the nature spirits who had appeared to him - almost as if one could see right through him. Grandpa didn't look any different and even smiled at Edgar. When he left the barn, Edgar couldn't wait to tell his grandma. She listened closely, nodding her head. "You're a great deal like your grandpa," Grandma Cayce said.

She paused and turned a stern eye toward young Edgar: "Don't be afraid of that power you have. Just don't misuse it." She admonished Edgar to stay on the straight and narrow and that God would show him the way to use his psychic abilities.

Edgar saw Grandpa Cayce on a number of occasions after he died and even had conversations with him. He realized that people had strange ideas about what is called death. He knew that death was merely leaving the body behind. His grandfather looked even better after he was dead than he did the day he died; he seemed to look younger.

An Angelic Encounter

When Edgar Cayce was ten years old, the family began taking him to the Liberty Christian Church in Hopkinsville, Kentucky, for Sunday services. Edgar felt immediately at home. He loved the minister's sermons, especially the stories about Jesus, and he wanted to know more about the Bible. Edgar's father, Leslie, was so impressed with his son's interest in religion he went to town and bought Edgar a Bible. By June 1887, six months after Edgar was given his Bible, he had read it from cover to cover. He didn't quite understand all that was in the

The Sleeping Prophet

Book, but one day he vowed that he would be an expert on the Scriptures.

Edgar wanted to read the Bible through once for every year of his life. The stories came alive for him, from the fall of Babylon to the Resurrection to the Book of Revelation; he read them again and again. He loved the New Testament best of all. He loved the stories of Jesus and His miracles.

One bright summer day when he was thirteen, Edgar took his Bible to his favorite secluded spot in the woods. As he finished the New Testament and began over again in the book of Genesis, Edgar noticed that the sunlight had dimmed considerably in the woods, as if someone had stepped in front of him, blocking the sun. He was startled to see that there indeed was someone standing in front of him. At first he thought the woman was his mother. As his eyes adjusted, however, he saw that the figure was more beautiful than anyone he had ever seen. There were rounded forms behind the woman's shoulders, which extended almost to the ground behind her.

Wings, Edgar thought. *Those are angels' wings.*

Just as this thought had passed through his mind, the woman before him smiled. "Your prayers have been heard," she said. "Tell me what you would like most of all, so that I may give it to you."

Edgar was paralyzed with fear and astonishment. *There's an angel in front of me.* He couldn't move. Couldn't speak. Couldn't do anything. After what felt like an eternity, Edgar heard his own voice as if he were speaking from very far away.

"I would like to be helpful to others, especially to children when they're sick."

Jesus had devoted His life to helping people, healing them, and He loved children. Edgar wanted to be helpful, too. He wanted to be a follower of Him, just like the minister at the church. Edgar wondered if the lady came because he wanted so much to understand the Bible.

She's not just a lady, Edgar thought. *Is she my guardian angel?*

Just as quickly as the lady appeared, she vanished before his eyes.

Edgar ran home to tell his mother what had happened. He worried he was losing his mind; maybe he was reading the Bible too much.

"You said you wanted to help people," his mother said. "That's not crazy. That's what we're here for. And why not? Why shouldn't an angel appear to you? You're a good boy."

Edgar felt gratitude and a little shy. He wasn't accustomed to praise. Edgar's mother speculated that perhaps he was going to be called for a high purpose. Perhaps he would become a doctor or a minister.

"You'll be something. That's for sure, Edgar."

The next day he felt tired, listless, bored. He couldn't concentrate in school. His mind and thoughts were wandering aimlessly. The teacher became exasperated when Edgar couldn't spell the word "cabin." It was an easy word for a thirteen-year-old boy. The teacher made Edgar stay after school and write "cabin" 500 times on the blackboard. After the tedious task, Edgar made his way home feeling more tired than ever.

Leslie Cayce was waiting for his son to return home from school. The schoolmaster had talked with him, saying how badly Edgar had done that day in school. Leslie wasted no time in reprimanding the boy when he got home.

"You sit in that chair," he ordered. "We're going to go over these spelling lessons until you get it right. This is a disgrace!" For the next three hours, Edgar tried and tried to spell the words his father commanded him to spell; it didn't seem to be of any use. He was in a fog. He couldn't remember the most basic lessons from school. This infuriated Leslie, and he berated his son, shouting at him, even knocking him out of his chair.

"You're going to spell these words right if we have to stay here all night," Leslie roared. Edgar was feeling so low and sad; he couldn't understand himself. As his father prepared to go back through the spelling book, Edgar heard a voice; it was very clear:

"Edgar, go to sleep on the book and we will help you." It was the voice of the lady, the angel, he had seen the day before.

Edgar pleaded with his father to let him rest for just a few minutes and look over the speller. He promised his father he would do better.

"Please. Just give me a few minutes."

Leslie reluctantly agreed with his son, handing him the spelling book, and left the room. Edgar put the book on the table and lay his head on it. He fell instantly asleep.

What seemed like a moment later, his father was shaking him. "Let's start again," Leslie said. Edgar rubbed the sleep from his eyes and sat up.

"Cabin."

"C-a-b-i-n." It was strange, but Edgar could actually *see* the word, picture-perfect in his mind. He could see the other words on the pages as well. Like in a photograph.

Leslie Cayce grew bewildered as his son accurately spelled every word he asked. Finally, he turned to the hardest words in the speller.

"Synthesis."

"S-y-n-t-h-e-s-i-s."

Leslie's bewilderment turned into anger. "What is this? We've been going through this book all night long and you couldn't spell anything. Now you can spell *everything*! Why?"

"I don't know," Edgar said. "I just went to sleep on the book and now I can see every word perfectly. Like a picture." Not only could Edgar spell every word in the book, he knew what page the words appeared on.

"You get to bed," his father growled, shaking his head. "I just don't understand this at all." Edgar obeyed his father and silently thanked the lady for helping him. S*he really must be an angel*, he thought.

From that time forward, Edgar went from being a below-average to exceptional student. His strange ability to gain knowledge from books by sleeping on them worked in every subject in school: arithmetic, history, even geography. Edgar retained in his mind a picture of the world's map in the book. He could identify every continent and country, and he could accurately name longitudes and latitudes, although he didn't know exactly what they were.

Leslie Cayce made an easy transition from being a bewildered father to a very proud father. He told everybody in Christian County that all his son had to do was sleep on his books to learn the lessons. Edgar was teased mercilessly by his classmates, and he wished that his father would keep his mouth shut.

Edgar's mother would only smile and nod when he told her stories about his peculiar abilities. She kept reminding him that he had been chosen for a special purpose.

A Modern-Day Mystic

The story of Edgar Cayce reads like the Bible stories in which God chooses some special person to be a prophet or a messenger. Only Edgar's mother had an inkling of the remarkable abilities her son would manifest years later after his angelic encounter while reading the Bible. Edgar was still quite young when he had an unusual experience which set the stage for what would eventually become a remarkable life's work.

In 1901, at the age of twenty-four, Edgar Cayce lost his voice. The ailment began as a cold, then developed into laryngitis, from which he couldn't recover. For more than a year, he couldn't speak above a hoarse whisper. Medical specialists were called in from all over the state of Kentucky to observe Edgar's malady. After examining his vocal chords, all the doctors announced that they were baffled: there was no hindrance or blockage in the vocal chords. As a last resort, a hypnotist was brought to the desperate Cayce. If there wasn't anything physically wrong with him, maybe there was something disturbing him mentally.

The thought bothered Edgar a great deal. He didn't *feel* particularly disturbed about anything. He deduced that hypnosis couldn't hurt him, although it was considered extremely controversial at the turn of the century. The procedure hadn't found its way into the medical mainstream, but was used more for entertainment: A hypnotist would call someone up to a stage and, after placing the person under hypnosis, would have that individual perform embarrassing acts, barking like a dog or crowing like a chicken. It was amazing to watch. People had no idea what they did or said while under hypnosis.

The Cayce family contacted one of these entertainer hypnotists, but he couldn't get Edgar to take a post-hypnotic suggestion in which he could regain the use of his voice. After several unsuccessful attempts to place Edgar into a deep trance state, a local osteopath, who had heard of Cayce's malady, decided on a new approach. As Edgar began to relax into the hypnotic sleep, Al Layne gave him a hypnotic suggestion with a twist: He told Edgar to look into his own body while in the hypnotic state and tell the people present what was wrong with him.

Gertrude Evans, who was Edgar's fiancée, his father, and the local physician were all anxiously watching the strange hypnosis session. Layne repeated the suggestion three times. Just as he was about to give Edgar the suggestion to wake up, thinking the session was a failure, Edgar began to speak.

"Yes, we have the body here," Edgar said. Gertrude nearly wept with joy. Those were the first clear words he had spoken in over a year.

"There is a constriction to the vocal chords due to stress," Edgar said in a deep sleep. "The circulation is impaired. Suggest that the body's circulation is returning to normal, and we will fix it."

Al Layne was startled. He'd never encountered anything of the kind before. *He's telling me to give him a post-hypnotic suggestion!* Without hesitation, he gave Edgar the suggestion:

"The circulation in the body of Edgar Cayce is now completely normal."

To the amazement of everyone in the room, Edgar's throat became a bright crimson red, the color rising like a thermometer. In a few seconds, the inflamed color subsided and he spoke: "Now give the body the suggestion to awaken."

Layne spoke to Edgar in gentle tones, suggesting that all of his internal organs were operating perfectly normal; he would count now from ten to one. When he reached one, Edgar would awaken.

" ... three ... two ... one. Edgar, you are now awake."

Edgar opened his eyes and stretched. He sat up abruptly and coughed, spitting out a glob of blood and mucus.

"Say something!" Layne demanded.

"Hello!" Edgar said perfectly clear. "Hello, everybody! Hey, I can talk again!" Gertrude hugged her future husband. The physician and Al Layne looked at one another in astonishment.

The doctor asked Edgar if he remembered anything from when he was under hypnosis. Cayce was thoughtful for a moment but couldn't recall. Then he asked how he got his voice back.

"*You* got your voice back," Layne said. Everyone in the room was looking at Edgar in amazement.

"Edgar, you talked just like a doctor," Layne said excitedly. "You mentioned stress and impaired circulation, and you told me to give you a post-hypnotic suggestion! I've never seen anything like it."

Edgar looked at Layne and laughed, feeling as if he was being put on. "I don't have the slightest idea what you're talking about," he said.

"I can see you don't," Layne said. "That's what makes this all the more amazing."

Gertrude and Edgar left the room, while the doctors stayed behind discussing the unusual hypnotic session. Layne wondered why he couldn't do it to diagnose other people's medical problems. He felt he stumbled onto something big. Later that afternoon, he asked if Edgar would mind going under hypnosis again.

The Sleeping Prophet

"Just as an experiment," Layne said.

"I don't know," Edgar said, feeling suspicious. "It's pretty strange for me not to know what I'm saying." He was thoughtful and a little worried. "I guess it won't hurt anything," he said at last, but he felt strangely out of control. *What if I say something crazy?* he thought. *Worse, what if I AM crazy?*

Before the second hypnotic session, Edgar told Layne that when he went under, he experienced a peculiar sensation just as he had when he was a boy and slept on his books. Edgar lay down on the couch, and Layne began the hypnotic session. When Layne felt that Edgar was sufficiently in the hypnotic sleep state, he gave the suggestion:

"Edgar, you will have before you Al Layne. Please look into this body of Al Layne and tell us what you find."

After a short period of silence, Edgar Cayce, the meagerly educated man from Christian County, seemed to become a knowledgeable physician. He described every major system of Layne's body: the autonomic nervous system, the digestive system. He even described an old injury of Layne's which had occurred years before, pinpointing the exact date. He used words Layne had only read in medical textbooks: "pneumogastric plexus," "spinal subluxations," "adhesions in the gall duct." After a very in-depth diagnosis, Edgar recommended that Layne have chiropractic adjustments to the spine. He even directed specific vertebrae which needed adjusting. Edgar also advised a change of diet and more exercise. Then in the same monotone voice, he said, "We are through for the present." Layne then gave Edgar the suggestion to wake up. Again, he stretched as if awaking from a deep sleep.

Layne was surprised to hear that once again Edgar didn't remember a word of what was said while he was under hypnosis. Edgar was surprised and more than a little disconcerted to learn that he accurately described Layne's physical problems and recommended a specific medical treatment.

"But I don't know anything about medicine," Edgar protested.

"You sure do when you're asleep," Layne said. "You're like a doctor when you're asleep."

The Sleeping Physician

The messages that Edgar Cayce would give in the sleep state came to be known as "readings." Although he was uneasy with this mysterious part of his psyche, he found himself in demand by the local medical doctors who were bringing their most difficult patients to his home. Usually the physicians contacted Al Layne, and then they would come to Edgar for a "psychic consultation." As before, Layne would relax Cayce through hypnotic suggestion and then ask him to psychically examine the physician's patient. Cayce's diagnoses were amazingly accurate. He even offered prescriptions and herbal remedies. If the remedy could not be purchased at a pharmacy, the sleeping Cayce would tell Layne how to prepare the prescription, complete with the required drams, ounces, and milligrams. He would tell the baffled physicians where to locate hard-to-find medical properties - sometimes mentioning the names and street addresses of pharmaceutical companies in other towns and states.

Layne would continually take notes during Cayce's readings and give the copy to the physicians, who would instruct their patients on carrying out the readings' recommendations. At first, the inquiring physicians kept the liaison with Cayce a secret, only giving the patients the medical orders without explanation. Eventually, however, word got out that Cayce was the one who was helping the local clientele get well. Soon, people began showing up at Edgar's home to thank him for restoring their health. Word began to spread about the "sleeping doctor" who could diagnose illness and recommend treatment. It didn't seem to matter if patients were "incurable," if they followed the readings' treatment regimen, they were healed in more than ninety percent of the cases.

Edgar continued to seek the counsel of his mother, who had always believed in his abilities. "I just wonder if this really is a gift from

The Sleeping Prophet

God," Cayce said. "People seem to be getting well from the information, but I don't know where the information is coming from."

Edgar's mother quoted the Bible: "'By their fruits ye shall know them.' Edgar, remember in the New Testament? 'The lame shall walk, the deaf shall hear, the blind shall receive their sight.' Just remember what happened to you as a boy, Edgar. You told that lady you wanted to help people."

The memory of his boyhood vision of the angel was still crystal clear, after all these years. His own words to her came back not to haunt, but to comfort him; the words he spoke to the angel who had appeared to him so many years before: *I want to be helpful, especially to children.*

"When you feel uneasy," Edgar's mother said, "just remember Aime Dietrich."

The memory of that hopeless little girl swirled through Edgar's restless thoughts. Her father said that Aime was now happy and fully recovered; a far cry from when Edgar first met her at her house in Hopkinsville. Aime had contracted a bad case of the flu three years before when she was two years old. Her fevers raged and then subsided. Now she couldn't talk, nor had her mind developed beyond the age of two. Aime walked and played sometimes, but she didn't respond to her environment or to the people around her; her mind was vacant. Convulsions, as many as twelve per day, had started a year after the attack of flu, resembling grand mal epilepsy. Specialists were called to the Dietrich home from all over the country. No one could help her. As a last resort, the parents institutionalized their daughter, hoping that around-the-clock care would bring her out of the strange malady. The best physicians in the country finally pronounced Aime hopelessly incurable.

Edgar met Mr. and Mrs. Dietrich and looked in on Aime, who was playing with blocks in the nursery. Al Layne then led Edgar into the den, where he lay down and went into a sleep state.

As Cayce's eyelids began to flutter, Layne read the hypnotic suggestion: "You will have before you Aime Dietrich, who is present in this house. You will carefully diagnose this body and recommend treatment."

After a moment, Edgar began to speak in the strange, monotone voice of sleep.

"Yes, we have the body here." At that point, Cayce became not only a remarkable physician, but seemed to travel through time and identified exactly when Aime's trouble began: Several days before contracting the flu, she had fallen from a horse-drawn carriage, injuring her tailbone. The combination of the spinal injury and the influenza was short-circuiting her nervous system, causing the seizures. Cayce specifically identified which vertebrae needed chiropractic realignment. Layne was to carry out the treatment. The language in which Cayce spoke was foreign to everyone in the room except Layne. At the close of the reading, however, Cayce gave a prognosis which caused Mrs. Dietrich to weep:

"As we find, the body will be well if the treatments are followed."

Layne followed Cayce's chiropractic recommendations. There was no noticeable change in Aime. Edgar went to sleep again, and Layne asked more questions. Edgar stated that Layne had not quite carried out the adjustments properly. He gave more specific instructions, which were carried out with greater precision. Within three months, Aime was completely healed. There was no recurrence of the seizures, and she was doing exceptionally well in school.

Edgar's wish expressed to the angel, to be helpful to children, was granted; yet he still felt uneasy. He didn't understand where the information came from and continued to worry about giving the readings. He warned Layne not to discuss the Dietrich case. Cayce had a photography business in Bowling Green to think about, and he and his new bride Gertrude were just beginning their lives together. He wanted to raise a family, teach Sunday school, and work in his garden.

The Sleeping Prophet

He would do all these things and more, but he would have to get over his uneasiness of giving readings. The needs of sick people would beckon him for the rest of his life. And he wasn't a person to turn anyone away.

It wasn't until Edgar's wife Gertrude became terminally ill with tuberculosis that he would seriously set aside his doubts about giving readings.

In 1910, when Gertrude contracted tuberculosis, they sought the advice of physicians and specialists and admitted her to the local hospital. Edgar would only consider using the readings as a last resort. In the end, the last resort was all he had left: The doctors pronounced Gertrude incurable and sent her home to die.

Cayce watched his ailing wife cough herself to exhaustion. There was nothing medically left to do for her. "Dear God," Edgar prayed, "if this power of mine is going to be of any help, let it help my wife." Edgar called in several local physicians who were skeptical, but at least sympathetic to the readings' advice. Edgar asked them to take notes during the reading session. After he entered into the sleep state, he began the process of psychically evaluating Gertrude's physical condition, giving detailed prescriptions and a treatment outline.

The doctors were more skeptical than ever: The sleeping Cayce had recommended a bizarre treatment which included a liquid formula of heroin to be given every day, a basic diet which was more alkaline-than acid-producing, and a strange contraption made of a charred oak keg into which was poured apple brandy. Gertrude wasn't to drink the potion, but to inhale the fumes which would rise to the top of the keg.

The combination of the charcoal and brandy fumes would heal the lung's tissue devastated by the tuberculosis germ and would in turn kill the tubercle itself.

When Cayce awoke from the reading, he saw that the TB specialist and all the physicians, except for his close friend Dr. Wesley Ketchum, were gone.

"They think you're a quack," Ketchum said. "None of them would prescribe a remedy with heroin."

Edgar was more distressed than ever. This reading was Gertrude's last hope! "Did the reading say she would recover?" Edgar asked.

Ketchum nodded, looking at this strange man who knew more about medicine than he did.

"Will you write the prescription?" Edgar asked.

"I will," Ketchum agreed.

After nearly eight months of the prescribed treatment and many follow-up readings from Cayce, Gertrude made a slow, but nevertheless complete recovery. This was the final confirmation he needed to go ahead with the readings for the rest of his life.

The Psychic Mind of Edgar Cayce

Al Layne, Dr. Ketchum, and Edgar's father Leslie wondered how the mechanics of the readings worked. After Cayce went to sleep on one occasion, they asked a series of questions.

"Edgar Cayce's mind is amenable to suggestion," the reading said, "the same as all other subconscious minds, but in addition thereto it has the power to interpret to the objective mind of others what it acquires *from the subconscious mind of other individuals* of the same kind ... The conscious mind receives the impression from without and transfers all thought to the subconscious, where it remains even though the conscious be destroyed [dies]."[4] (Author's italics)

In essence, when Cayce laid aside his conscious mind while giving a reading, a part of his unconscious or superconscious mind traveled through time and space and "read" the mental and physical pattern of the individual requesting the information, from his or her own subconscious mind. Cayce could also "read" from the souls and spirits no longer in the material world. This was possible because, although the conscious mind or personality-self dies, the subconscious self lives on and survives physical death. Cayce said that the subconscious mind is the "record" of all experiences, thoughts, feelings, etc. At the point of death, this "memory" of the soul becomes the conscious mind of the soul. At times, certain individuals whom the Cayce family had known would project messages through the readings, identifying themselves.

A reading was given on the health of Hugh Lynn Cayce, the eldest son of Edgar, and it had a different tone from other readings. There was a distinct personality delivering the information. At the end of the reading, the message was given, "This is Hill." Gertrude Cayce immediately knew now why the information seemed familiar: Dr. Hill had been Hugh Lynn's physician in Hopkinsville and had died since the Cayces moved to Bowling Green.

Because all people are linked together by the subconscious mind - the living and the dead - those conducting the readings found that the individuals did not have to be present for Edgar Cayce to give a reading on them; he only needed their name and address. Cayce's psychic ability is today called clairvoyance - the ability to retrieve information from distances without being physically present where he was giving the readings.

Edgar Cayce Taps the Universal Mind

After twenty-three years of giving physical readings for people, it was discovered that Cayce could give readings on any subject, not just health problems. This understanding opened up a whole new dimension to Cayce's work; the small group of Cayce's friends and family asked the sleeping psychic about the nature of God, dreams, prophecy, comparative religions, humanity's origin, purpose, and destiny on the earth, as well as about angels and archangels.

Regardless of the type of reading Cayce gave, he seemed to

completely lay aside his personality-self and respond from the sleep state in the plural "we": "We have the body here ... as we find the physical conditions are disturbed ... We are through with this reading."

Exactly who were the we the readings spoke of?

Cayce's unconscious mind seemed to tap into the very "mind" and memory of the universe, giving detailed information of eons past, the lost years of Jesus, the earth's history that was previously labeled "prehistoric." According to the readings, the "we" was a universal source of all knowledge to which Cayce's mind became attuned; it was not necessarily entities or persons, but a unity of forces which included the soul-mind of Edgar Cayce. There was no limit to the questions Cayce could answer while in the sleep state. Certain information, however, would not be given if the seeker was interested merely for curiosity's sake. On those occasions (which were rare), Cayce would say, "This must be found in self ... " or " ... this may not be given ... "

At times, the sleeping Cayce reminded those conducting the readings to always have a high, selfless purpose when they sought information and guidance from them. That unselfish purpose served as a sort of mystical "antenna," providing Cayce a clear channel through which he could "tune in" to the information desired. The phenomenon operated very much like a radio receiver. When a person was seeking with a sincerity of purpose, the psychic readings would be given from the highest source possible.

Much of the readings' accuracy had to do with the desire of the individual requesting help or information. If the requestor was a doubter or a skeptic, only seeking information for curiosity's sake, the readings became inaccurate or vague. At the same time, if a sincerity of purpose was held by an individual or a group of people, then Cayce was able to give inspiring information, presenting an unlimited reservoir of spiritual knowledge to the inquirers.

The Sleeping Prophet

In fact, if the attunement of the group or person requesting information was clear, a divine messenger would speak through the sleeping Cayce. From this information, many people came to understand the larger influence of the angels among human beings. The readings affirmed that the world was about to enter a spiritual renaissance period. A period where communion with angels would not be unusual at all, but instead would be part of the greater plan to awaken humanity to its divine origins.

Chapter 3

Divine Intervention

"And then shall he send his angels, and shall gather together his elect from the four winds, from the uttermost part of the earth to the uttermost part of heaven." - Mark 13:27

The Archangel Michael

OF the over 14,000 readings Cayce gave in his lifetime, 116 have come to be called "work readings." Those messages meticulously detail how Cayce's associates should carry out the spiritual as well as the day-to-day business of managing his work. This collection speaks not only of how the readings should be used to benefit people, they also discuss the larger scope of *why* Cayce's psychic ability manifested: "For the time has arisen in the earth when men - everywhere - seek to know more of the mysteries of the mind, the soul, the *soul's* mind ... "[5]

Cayce's role was as a channel through which those "mysteries" might be given. In his day, the collective consciousness of humanity had evolved to a point where the secrets of the universe would be sought after, not only by the mystics and sages, but by everyday people. Cayce alluded that as the twentieth century unfolded, more and more people would seek to understand themselves as souls. Other readings predicted that the "spiritual forces" - which include angels - would be more interactive with humankind, prompting a global spiritual awakening. The spiritual forces may be described as a collective reservoir of divine intelligence, whose mission it is to inspire, lead, and direct people to a conscious spiritual awareness. As we've seen, these divine intelligences sometimes operate as angels who assist us in times of distress.

The readings contain fascinating material on how angels operate in our lives. At times their influence comes as an outward experience, such as Cayce had when he was a boy, in which he actually saw an angel. At other times, angelic experiences come as inspirations or emotions, such as suddenly not feeling alone while being *physically* alone. Often angels present themselves to us as inner reassurances through intuition or in dreams or visions. Such experiences serve to remind us that there is a greater spiritual reality within us than we may have ever considered before.

The Cayce readings indicate that the phenomenon of divine intervention by angels is directing us to a higher calling, a return to the Source or God. One curious gentleman who came to Cayce was fascinated with psychic development. He took his seeking "to know more of the *mysteries* of the mind" very seriously indeed and obtained readings from Cayce on how he might become psychic. In fact, he wanted to know the basis of the highest psychic experience that he could have on earth. After a short dissertation on the spiritual aspects of life, Cayce's response to his question didn't direct the man to the mechanics of psychic ability, such as telepathy or clairvoyance, but stated instead a divine truth:

"[The highest possible psychic realization is] that God, the Father, speaks directly to the sons of men - even as He has promised."[6]

The angels are one of the ways that God "speaks directly" to us, as shown by the stories in chapter 1. The readings of Edgar Cayce as well as the inspired writings and lectures of Rudolf Steiner, Helene Blavatsky, and so many others are additional channels through which these spiritual reminders have come. If these sources are anything at all, they confirm that spiritual help is available to us; voices in the wilderness which confirm that humankind is an integral, vital, intimate part of One Creative Force. These are all old voices in a new age. Most of the time we only realize a sense of divine communion in a time of crisis. But God is still at work, crisis or not.

Divine Intervention

Just as in biblical times, when men and women were chosen to be channels or messengers of the Divine, Cayce and his small group of helpers were told in the "work readings" that they had been gathered together for a high spiritual purpose - not to form a new religion or cult, but to help bring humanity's spiritual awareness back to the forefront of the world's thinking. The readings themselves indicated that this information would be of benefit "to the individual, the group, the classes, the masses ... "[7]

As if to punctuate the importance of the scope of divine intervention, an extraordinary phenomenon occurred during a reading in 1928. It was the first time Archangel Michael spoke through the sleeping Cayce.

Michael the Archangel Speaks

On July 15, 1928, the group was in the midst of receiving a reading announcing the ideal and purpose of the Cayce association: "That we may make manifest the love of God and man." Suddenly, Cayce made an unusual introduction for an unseen guest who would speak through him many times over the next fifteen years.

"HARK!" Cayce said abruptly in the sleep state. "There comes the voice of one who would speak to those gathered here... " Suddenly the sleeping, monotone voice of Edgar Cayce boomed out a message, no longer speaking in the universal language of "we," but in the startling persona of "I":

> "I AM MICHAEL, LORD OF THE WAY! BEND THY HEAD, O YE CHILDREN OF MEN! GIVE HEED UNTO THE WAY AS IS SET BEFORE YOU IN THAT SERMON ON THE MOUNT, IN THAT ON YON HILL THIS ENLIGHTENMENT MAY COME AMONG MEN ... FOR IN ZION THY NAMES ARE WRITTEN, AND IN SERVICE WILL COME TRUTH!"[8]

The "hill" referred to the hill in Virginia Beach where the group was attempting to establish one of the first holistic hospitals in the country. Years later, the eldest son of Edgar Cayce, Hugh Lynn, who was present for this reading, vividly recounted the day this cryptic message was given:

"After an in-depth study of Dad's readings, I accepted the fact that the work was indeed guided by what I call the 'Divine Unseen Forces.' Given the number of people who were helped physically from his readings, this powerful message from Michael assured me that the information in the readings was - for the most part - coming from the highest spiritual sources. I consider Michael the Archangel to be one of the direct voices or manifestations of God."

When Michael's message was given through Cayce, Hugh Lynn said that his father's voice did not change in diction or dialect, as is often the case with trance mediums who channel discarnate spirits. The intensity and volume, however, with which the messages were given was overwhelming.

"Michael's message was given with such force that I could hear the windows rattling in their frames in our home," Hugh Lynn said. "I could even hear the cups rattling in the dish-drainer in the kitchen. The vibrations nearly knocked us all out of our chairs."

Who is Michael and what did his message say to the small group gathered in Virginia Beach? Hugh Lynn asked this question in a later reading, and the sleeping Cayce said that "Michael is an archangel that stands before the throne of the Father ... Michael is the lord or the guard of the change that comes in every soul that seeks the [spiritual] way, even as in those periods when His manifestations came in the earth."[9]

Archangel Michael (whose name in Hebrew translates to "who is like God?"), called Saint Michael in the Christian churches, is one of a group of archangels known in Judaism, Christianity, and Islam. In the Old Testament, a prophetic reference to Michael in the book of Daniel seems to coincide with his messages in the Cayce readings. "And at that time shall Michael stand up," Scripture says, " ... the great prince which standeth for the children of thy people: and there shall be a time of trouble, such as never was since there was a nation even to that same time: and at that time thy people shall be delivered, every one that shall be found written in the book. And many of them that sleep in the dust of the earth shall awake ... " (Daniel 12:1-2)

This prophetic passage coincides with Michael's message through Cayce in 1928: "for in Zion thy names are written." Unity church founder Charles Fillmore defined Zion as "Love's abode in the phase of the subjective consciousness where high, holy thoughts and ideals abide."[10] Zion, in this case, represents a spiritual state of consciousness.

Michael's message in the readings also should be seen as a "wake-up call" for all of us. As the prophetic biblical verse of Daniel indicates, the current days of our century *are* troublesome. Sociologists, psychologists, and the clergy are saying that the immense challenges facing us now are unsurpassed: critical environmental issues, social and political upheavals, soaring crime rates, and earth changes. And yet, the Cayce readings consider these as signs of the times of change predicted in the Bible, the forerunners of events of great upheaval which the readings say will bear out Jesus' prediction:

"And when ye shall hear of wars and rumours of wars, be ye not troubled: for such things must needs be; but the end shall not be yet ... nation shall rise against nation ... and there shall be earthquakes in divers places, and there shall be famines and troubles ... " (Mark 13:7-8)

Michael is an archangel of *change*, of movement to higher consciousness in thought as well as spirit. Cayce defined Michael's role in the spiritual and mental evolvement of humanity: " ... Michael is the Lord of the Way - and in the ways of understanding, of conception, of bringing about those things that make for the changes in the attitudes in physical, mental or material relationships, is the *guide* through such spiritual relations ... "[11] This archangel's role in our time is vitally important - for Michael helps humankind to harken and listen to the higher spiritual calling.

His manifestation in this age is a sign of light in the midst of the darkness; it is a divine reassurance as well as a call for each of us. Rather than fear the great upheavals, we should spiritually prepare ourselves. Often when various religious groups speak of biblical prophecy being fulfilled in our time, there is a tendency to concentrate on the "labor" the world is enduring and not the eventual "birth." It's easy to point to all the problems of a world in crisis. That the nightly news broadcasts within the U.S. are grim is an understatement. Our world and the national media depend upon the negative reporting of news for ratings; bad news sells. But the Cayce readings tell us that the outcome of this crisis is our responsibility. Our thoughts, feelings, perceptions, and our activities will ultimately create the future. How we collectively visualize the future will come about in our personal lives.

Archangel Michael is a messenger who calls upon us to be hopeful for these times - regardless of how the outward appearance of the world defines itself. It is too limited a view to say that these angelic pronouncements of Michael were directed only to those among Cayce's group. The words of the "Lord of the Way" are for everyone who seeks to be a part of this spiritual renaissance in our present ages. Since recorded time, Michael the Archangel has been a leader, way-shower, advisor, beckoning the souls of the earth to remember their spiritual source.

According to *The Book of Enoch*, which chronicles the mystical meeting of the prophet Enoch with the archangels, Michael and his command of faithful troops waged a war against Archangel Lucifer and his followers, casting them into hell. According to the Christian seer and mystic Rudolf Steiner, that war represents the archetypal struggle between good and evil *within* us. The good is represented by Michael, the darkness represented by Satan. Steiner believed that

Archangel Michael is the guardian of the nations of the world at the close of this age and the beginning of the new millennium. He believed that Michael is a harbinger, bringing humanity to an understanding of Christ or "God incarnated within us." The cosmic drama between the high forces of Michael and Satan (the Dragon) are reflected within the psyches and souls of every one incarnated in the earth; we each must choose between good and evil. In a lecture given in Austria in 1923, Steiner made some interesting points about Michael the "outer" archangel and the "inner" guardian, both real and active spiritual intelligences.

" ... Michael stands cosmically behind man," he said, "while within man there is an etheric image of Michael that wages the real battle through which man can gradually become free; for it is not Michael himself who wages the battle, but human devotion and the resulting image of Michael. In the cosmic Michael there still lives that being to whom men can look up and who engaged in the original cosmic struggle with the Dragon."[12]

The movement of Michael's influence in the affairs of humanity is like the sunlight that breaks across the face of the earth in the darkness. The readings define darkness as a symbol of spiritual ignorance, and the light is the spiritual realization of the soul and its connection with God. Michael, the spiritual guardian and way-shower for humanity in this age, is radiating an awakening not only from within us, but from the unseen realms to the earth realm. According to Cayce's readings, the dawn of this awakening is what we're approaching in consciousness in the new millennium.

Christ Consciousness Returns

Christ Consciousness is defined as the awareness of the soul's oneness with God imprinted in pattern on the mind, and the Cayce readings indicate that it will begin to be the ruling force in the earth by 1998. This awareness has always been available for us at the soul level, but it has not been able to be comprehended *en masse* until now through the collective will of humanity. Michael's role as the guardian is to direct and awaken the spiritually sleeping souls of humanity to that reality. There was a time, however, in the earth's history when souls knew and remembered their spiritual origins (see chapter 7, "The Angelic Promise - From Adam to Jesus"). That era, a time when souls communed with the angelic forces and received direct conscious guidance from God, is now considered mythological and prehistoric.

The Cayce readings say that this period occurred before time as we know it, even before the earth, began. In that age, souls relied directly upon the spiritual hierarchies for guidance and direction. In the earth's evolution, humanity gradually became so distracted and enmeshed by the material world, social striving, and pursuing creature comforts, etc., that the channel for communion with the angelic forces became clouded, and eventually humans doubted there ever was such a channel available. We descended so far into materiality we didn't even suspect that we were out of touch with our spiritual origins! Today, messages are being given to a new generation from the same archangels who spoke to the old generations written about in the Bible. The times may be different, but the call is essentially the same: *Remember where you came from and who you are. You are one with God, and I am here to guide you.* But we must acknowledge this beckoning, believe in it, for it to be a part of our consciousness.

Archangel Michael and the Bible

Cayce's psychic ability was a valuable resource in identifying when in the biblical days of the New Testament Archangel Michael was active. In a biographical reading on the life of Jesus, information was given that it was the archangel Michael, in Matthew 1:20, who appeared to Joseph, the husband of Mary, in a dream after he doubted her immaculate conception: " ... behold, the angel of the Lord appeared unto him in a dream, saying, Joseph, thou son of David, fear not to take unto thee Mary thy wife: for that which is conceived in her is of the Holy Ghost."

Divine Intervention

Michael, confirmed by Cayce in a reading to have been the divine messenger, came to bear witness that Mary had immaculately conceived the Messiah. This story correlates with Steiner's belief that the archangel Michael helped prepare the way for the appearance of Christ on earth 2,000 years ago. According to Cayce's readings, it was Michael who served as protector of Jesus and His parents, manifesting at least two more times in the dreams of Joseph.

Shortly after Jesus' birth at the time of Herod's edict, when he ordered all male children two years old and under to be put to death, the archangel Michael warned the Holy Family to flee to Egypt: "behold, the angel of the Lord appeareth to Joseph in a dream, saying, Arise, and take the young child and his mother, and flee into Egypt, and be thou there until I bring thee word: for Herod will seek the young child to destroy him."(Matthew 2:13) Joseph, Mary, and Jesus did escape to Egypt and were safe while the edict was being carried out. Michael again appeared to Joseph in a dream, ten years after their flight to Egypt, saying, "take the young child and his mother, and go into the land of Israel: for they are dead which sought the young child's life."(Matthew 2:20) According to Cayce, Herod had perished from cancer, and Michael alerted Joseph to return to Israel.

Archangel Michael and the Work of Cayce

Archangel Michael's appearances to the prophet Daniel and again to Joseph, indicate that his influence is active during critical times surrounding important spiritual changes. He appears to warn, confirm, admonish, and give guidance. The essence of Michael's messages in the Cayce readings contains all of these elements. His pronouncements emphasized that Cayce's work was a continuation of Christ's work. Indeed, as was Cayce's youthful wish granted by the angel, his readings continue to help countless thousands who seek to be healed of physical illness. They also shed light upon the spiritual destiny of the human soul.

The physical readings alone had demonstrated a promise the Master gave 2,000 years ago: "the works that I do shall he do also; and greater works than these shall he do."(John 14:12) For of the people who had come into contact with Cayce's physical readings, the blind had received their sight, the deaf heard, the lame walked. Many of the people who had received healing through following Cayce's advice would state in testimonials that their healing was nothing short of a miracle; modern medicine pronounced many of them incurable, even Cayce's wife Gertrude. These people, once well, often tried to give credit to Edgar Cayce himself.

"If I am anything at all," Edgar would counter, "I am a channel through which the information comes. Nothing more or less." Cayce himself marveled when he read Archangel Michael's messages. Yet, as Hugh Lynn said, Cayce attributed the messages to those seeking guidance through the readings, that their desire to be divinely guided in this work was heard, and it was a sign along the way that they were on the right track.

In 1928, a close associate of Cayce's who had received numerous readings, wrote to him after examining the first Michael message: "The reading certainly was a wonderful demonstration, and I should have liked to have been there. While I have never doubted the correctness of the messages or the truth contained [in the readings] and the reality of our work, still it is heartening to feel the assurances come through so strongly."[13]

It is well to remember that Cayce needed such an assurance about his work. Although he had dedicated his life to serving and helping others through the readings, there was still the persistent unease that plagued him, worrying that somehow he might prescribe the wrong remedy or hurt someone. Archangel Michael helped Cayce understand that the direction of the readings was in the hands of the Divine.

Michael's messages, however, did not mean that Cayce and his associates would not face difficult days. Many problems arose in the work of the Cayce Hospital. After numerous personnel and investment conflicts, the Cayce Hospital closed. As shocking and disappointing as the closure was, the evidence was clear that during the hospital's brief life of two years, many people were completely healed.

Had Archangel Michael been wrong that "on yon hill this enlightenment may come among men"? No. While the hospital itself closed and the building subsequently had various owners, the work of Cayce continued on in the Association for Research and Enlightenment, Inc., which Cayce founded in 1931. In 1956, the Association reacquired the building, which now houses its administrative offices. The new organization kept the ideal to "make manifest the love of God and man" and set the stage for a new area of the work which would spiritually change the lives of thousands of people, even into the present day.

Cayce and his group decided to search for the spiritual meaning of life through a series of instructional readings that came to be known as the "Search for God" readings. They were eventually compiled into two books entitled *A Search for God*. Cayce's close group of associates and family wanted to know how they, too, could be of help to people as he had been. Could they become psychic like Cayce? Was it something they could learn? Over the course of eleven years, the group would receive instructions from the sleeping Cayce through his readings on how they could fulfill their soul's purposes. Each instruction or lesson built upon the next, gradually awakening the group to the truth that spirituality must be of practical use in life if it is to be of any worth.

During this time of spiritual unfoldment through the readings, on September 4, 1932, Archangel Michael again came through as he had in 1928. Michael reaffirmed that it was the *spiritual* work which was of vital importance - not necessarily a hospital or physical institution. As before, Cayce's monotone voice leaped to a crescendo; the universal "we" of the readings was absent as the divine messenger commanded the group:

"BE STILL, MY CHILDREN! BOW THINE HEADS, THAT THE LORD OF THE WAY MAY MAKE KNOWN UNTO YOU THAT HAVE BEEN CHOSEN FOR A SERVICE IN THIS PERIOD WHEN THERE IS THE NEED OF THAT SPIRIT BEING MADE MANIFEST IN THE EARTH, THAT THE WAY MAY BE KNOWN TO THOSE THAT SEEK THE LIGHT! FOR THE GLORY OF THE FATHER WILL BE MADE MANIFEST THROUGH YOU THAT ARE FAITHFUL UNTO THE CALLING WHEREIN THOU HAST BEEN CALLED! YE THAT HAVE NAMED THE NAME MAKE KNOWN IN THY DAILY WALKS OF LIFE, IN THE LITTLE ACTS OF THE LESSONS THAT HAVE BEEN BUILDED IN THINE OWN EXPERIENCE, THROUGH THOSE ASSOCIATIONS OF SELF IN MEDITATION AND PRAYER, THAT HIS WAY MAY BE KNOWN AMONG MEN: FOR HE CALLS ALL - WHOSOEVER WILL MAY COME - AND HE STANDS AT THE DOOR OF THINE OWN CONSCIENCE, THAT YE MAY BE AWARE THAT THE SCEPTER HAS NOT DEPARTED FROM ISRAEL, NOR HAVE HIS WAYS BEEN IN VAIN: FOR TODAY, WILL YE HARKEN, THE WAY IS OPEN - I, MICHAEL, CALL ON THEE!"[14]

Again, Michael confirms that these people "have been chosen" at a time "when there is the need" for a spiritual renewal in the earth. The ages may pass, but again and again there is the beckoning of the angels to humanity.

The reference to Israel is also important in Michael's message. This is not referring to the nation, but the readings state that Israel identifies all spiritual seekers who attempt to understand their relationship to God and magnify that understanding in their lives. All those who seek to bring spiritual awareness into their material lives are a part of Israel. This message was given in a reading defining Israel in a new light:

"In the application does the knowledge come of what is to be accomplished by self, in the step by step, line by line, that others may know of that promise that is to each individual that may be one with Him. Be not unmindful that those met in the way are seekers also, and are the Israel of the Lord."[15]

This broader definition of "seekers" after truth represents an awe-inspiring implication: All people of all spiritual and religious walks of life are a part of "Israel," and those who seek after spiritual truth are part of the dawning spiritualization now taking place in our world. The cryptic section of the message is "the scepter has not departed from Israel."

Edgar Cayce commented on the scepter in Israel during his Bible class in 1939. " … it was prophesied by Jacob that the scepter would not depart from Judah (Jacob's son) till Shiloh come, which is to say Judah's descendants would be the material channel for the birth of the Redeemer of the world [Christ]."[16] Jesus said in the New Testament that "This generation shall not pass away … "(Luke 21:32) until all these things are fulfilled. The readings indicate that the "generation" is a group of souls who are returning to help fulfill the earth's spiritual destiny: the reuniting in consciousness of humanity with God.

The readings gave additional details about Israel being a soul group and not necessarily a physical race:

"Israel is the chosen of the Lord," the sleeping Cayce said, "and that His promises, His care, His love, has not departed from those that seek to know His way, that seek to see His face … This is the meaning, this should be the understanding to all. Those that seek are Israel … Know, then, the scepter, the promise, the love, the glory of the Lord has not departed from them that seek His face!"[17]

Lecturer Mark Batten, a Unity church counselor and a former Catholic priest living in Virginia Beach, Virginia, has made an in-depth study of Archangel Michael's messages in the Cayce readings. In a private interview, he shared some insights about the nature of Michael and the archangels.

"The archangels - specifically Michael - do the direct biddings of God," Batten explained. "Cayce said that God is personal and impersonal; universal and individual. Archangels can lead nations to enlightenment as well as lead individuals to a divine awakening. Their job seems to be to draw people back to the awareness of God.

"Michael is not an entity or person as we have a tendency to think about angels; but he is a force, a vast spiritual energy - a divine intelligence. The archangels do not exchange in dialogue with people on earth per se, they only know to command whatever God desires and commands. They are too vast for *individual exchange*."

In essence, the archangels are messengers from God. Mark Batten had been a witness to the Michael messages given through another psychic. The psychic, who asked not to be identified, was able to go into trance as Edgar Cayce did.

"The voice of the person through whom Michael spoke just boomed," Batten said. "The messages are always similar to those given in the Cayce readings, always admonishing those present to hold fast to high spiritual principles, that this is a critical time in the earth's history. And that call is for *each one of us*. The Cayce readings indicate that each person who is in the earth for the close of the old and the beginning of the new millennium has chosen to be here for high spiritual reasons. We're all a part of it."

Batten also had experienced the windows rattling in their frames when Michael spoke through the psychic.

"The vibrations of the archangels are so powerful. It is loud, yes; but it is more the power than the volume that is overwhelming." The former priest gave an interesting analogy: an archangel operates at 15,000 volts, like an electrical current. A human being is operating at 120 volts. When such a force or a power like an archangel manifests itself, as Michael did through Cayce, it affects not just the channel, but the people in the room as well as the physical surroundings. "I knew I was in the presence of the Divine," he added.

Divine Intervention

Batten said that the psychic through which Michael's messages came remembered nothing of the experience. Did Edgar Cayce remember anything of the Michael encounters?

"No," Hugh Lynn said. "It was just like any other reading - he remembered nothing of the reading itself. Sometimes he would have dreams or visions; sometimes he would recall that he was speaking with or to someone during the reading. These experiences were not always pleasant for him. Sometimes the things that happened to him during a reading disquieted him a great deal."

On October 2, 1932, Edgar Cayce had one such experience following a message given by Archangel Michael which said:

> "HARK! O YE CHILDREN OF MEN! BOW THINE HEADS, YE SONS OF MEN: FOR THE GLORY OF THE LORD IS THINE, WILL YE BE FAITHFUL TO THE TRUST THAT IS PUT IN EACH OF YOU! KNOW IN WHOM YE HAVE BELIEVED! KNOW THAT HE IS LORD OF *ALL*, AND HIS WORD FAILETH NOT TO THEM THAT ARE FAITHFUL DAY BY DAY: FOR I, MICHAEL, WOULD PROTECT THOSE THAT SEEK TO KNOW HIS FACE!"[18]

Gladys Davis Turner was Edgar Cayce's longtime secretary, who transcribed the readings verbatim as Cayce gave them from 1923 until his death in 1945. At the end of Michael's message, she wrote an ominous note:

"Tears, silence, and beautiful attunement followed above reading. Edgar Cayce had a vision during the reading, had to leave the room a while; said he saw each of us as we should be and as we are."[19]

Evidently during the time that Michael was speaking through Cayce, Cayce was in such a high state of spiritual attunement that he had glimpsed the group members in their perfected, invisible, spiritually pure state. Gradually, as he sunk back into his day-to-day consciousness, he saw the images of material attachment, problems, habits of the group members - the general things that beset all human beings. First, he had seen the essential pureness of the soul, then he experienced the dross of material life, in their auras. This was a shock to Cayce, especially because of his waking sensitivity.

Archangel Michael's above message was one of encouragement and reassurance, for those people who were learning to apply spiritual principles had the promise of the Most High that they would be guided and directed in their important work.

The Archangel Michael in the Work of Nancy Fullwood

In 1917, American psychic and author Nancy Fullwood found herself listening to an inner voice which directed her to write. This voice was very kind and soothing. She undertook an experiment and felt herself "divide," as if part of her were watching herself and the other were observing her from a vantage point outside her body. She began taking dictation on the messages which came to her. Eventually, these writings became books - *The Tower of Light, The Flaming Sword*, and *The Song of Sano Tarot* - which were popular in the 1930s.

Of particular interest to the study of angels is that Fullwood began receiving very powerful messages in which Archangel Michael directed her writings. During these messages she felt herself enveloped in a white light which held an incredible energy. She never saw Michael, but felt his presence. The messages from him, which began in 1917, are strikingly similar to the discourses found in the Cayce readings. One message in particular predicts the oncoming shift in consciousness from the material to the spiritual:

> "I, Michael, lord of the Sun, have wrapped my mantle of light about the dark planet Earth. Through the action of my Fire, Earth will be purified and regenerated ... The old chaotic Earth will fall into oblivion and a new Earth, or state of consciousness, will rise out of it. Dwell not upon material disaster, for I say to you that conditions will exist in this new world [that] will be of

such beauty and harmony that the old world will be forgotten in the joy of the new life ... The old material world is even now beginning to recede upon itself and it will fall under its own chaos ... Listen deep within yourselves and you will know that I speak truth when I say that the children of light will not be conscious of the wind and the raging storm, for in their center, there is peace ... I, Michael, have spoken."[20]

Archangel Michael's message clearly indicates how human consciousness itself is evolving from the material to the spiritual again. So consistent are the force and style of Michael's messages through Cayce that it's easy to believe that the angelic messages are one and the same.

The Watchful Taskmaster

Archangel Michael's messages through Cayce were sometimes admonishing. In 1940, Cayce agreed to give a series of business readings attempting to locate oil wells in Texas. It seemed like a positive venture; the money would go to aid the Cayce work as well as other nonprofit organizations. At least that was the original intent. However, the readings given seemed mysteriously inaccurate; the proper oil well site could not be located; there were hindrances all along the way. There seemed to be something askew, but no one could find the reason or the culprit.

In one of the last oil well readings, the question was asked: "Can information be given at this time regarding the seeming inaccuracies in previous information regarding the production in the present [oil well drilling site]?"

The answer startled everyone in the room as the voice of Archangel Michael reprimanded those present:

"COME! HARKEN YE CHILDREN OF MEN! BOW THINE HEADS, YE SONS OF MEN! FOR I, MICHAEL, WOULD SPEAK WITH THEE CONCERNING THOSE

THINGS YE QUESTION HERE! HAVE YE NOT SEEN AND HEARD - UPON THE COURSE THAT IS PURSUED IN THE SEARCH THROUGH THIS MAN [Edgar Cayce] FOR KNOWLEDGE - IN SUCH YE DEVIATE AT THAT DEVELOPMENT OF MATERIALITY IN MAN'S SEARCH FOR GOD?"[21]

The warning was clear that their seeking information about an oil well through Cayce was at cross-purposes for which he had the ability to give readings. Michael even went so far as to say that such questioning deviated from the material Cayce should be giving. Shortly after this message, the oil well venture was abandoned as a failure.

On occasion, the warnings and admonitions from Archangel Michael had to be given to the very people who were governing Cayce's work. In the latter years of his life, Cayce was overworked and tired. *There Is a River*, his biography by Thomas Sugrue, had been published, resulting in thousands of letters and requests for readings. Additional office staff had to be hired to answer the correspondence and the telephones. In 1944, a year before Cayce's death, the office of the Association was particularly stressful. Reading appointments were booked *two years in advance,* people were showing up at his door from all over the country, desperate for him to give a reading to save a dying relative or friend. The atmosphere surrounding the work was chaotic; the office staff were fighting and bickering. Cayce himself was pushed to the brink of exhaustion. Earlier "work readings" told him to have only two reading periods per day; the first at 10:30 to 11:30 a.m., the second at 3:30 to 4:30 p.m. To attempt to do more than that, the readings warned, would endanger Cayce's life. Nevertheless, the letters from the thousands who needed his help haunted the waking Cayce. His temper grew short, his strength was waning - still he attempted to give readings.

"You're killing yourself, Edgar," his wife said. "You've got to slow

Divine Intervention

down."

Cayce walked to the back room of their house which served as the mail room, dumped out one of the burlap mail bags stuffed to the brim with letters and cards pleading for his help.

"How can I turn them away?" Edgar asked, searching his wife's eyes. "How can I *not* push myself?" It was a pathetic moment. "It kills me not to do the readings. If I overdo it, that will kill me, too."

Exhausted, spent, and feeling helpless, Edgar knew his fate.

"I've got to do it till I can't do it any more," he said finally. "That's all."

From the latter part of 1943 through 1944, Cayce sometimes held six to eight separate reading periods *a day*. On several instances, because of his demanding schedule and the stressful office environment, he was unable psychically to "connect" with the information. He couldn't obtain information through the readings *at all*.

One of the last readings ever given was on his own failing health. Because of his poor physical condition, it was given in a whisper. Cayce's words were nearly inaudible as he lay on his couch. Gladys Davis had to strain to hear the reading in order to transcribe it in shorthand. It confirmed that Cayce's health was indeed going downhill, brought on not only by physical and mental exhaustion, but by the infighting of the office staff which was hindering his ability as well.

Suddenly, in the midst of the reading, Cayce's wispy voice was replaced by the powerful voice of the Archangel Michael. He commanded one of the harshest messages ever recorded in the readings:

> "BOW THINE HEADS, YE CHILDREN OF MEN! FOR I, MICHAEL, LORD OF THE WAY, WOULD SPEAK WITH THEE! YE GENERATION OF VIPERS, YE ADULTEROUS GENERATION, BE WARNED! THERE IS TODAY BEFORE

THEE GOOD AND EVIL! CHOOSE THOU WHOM YE WILL SERVE! WALK IN THE WAY OF THE LORD! OR ELSE THERE WILL COME THAT SUDDEN RECKONING, AS YE HAVE SEEN! BOW THINE HEADS, YE WHO ARE UNGRACIOUS, UNREPENTANT! FOR THE GLORY OF THE LORD IS AT HAND! THE OPPORTUNITY IS BEFORE THEE! ACCEPT OR REJECT! BUT DON'T BE PIGS!"[22]

Theologian and psychologist Harmon H. Bro, Ph.D., was present for that reading. He interpreted the "reckoning" of which Michael spoke as being the gradual waning of Cayce's ability to give readings. Bro said those present in the room felt the reprimand from Michael to the very depths of their souls. In his reflective Cayce biography, *A Seer Out of Season*, he writes about what they felt after they received the message:

"As the [reading] ended, all of us were weeping. I looked around at anguished, pale faces. Nobody spoke. We each rose quickly to leave ... It did not matter to me exactly who the voice had been that called itself Michael. Whether a creation of Cayce's biblically formed mind, a discarnate being dismayed at our behavior ... or a genuine angelic presence, it had come into our midst not to bring blessing or to honor us, but to express burning rebuke. If this really were an archangel, I never wanted to deal with one again."[23]

Angelic Reassurance in Times of Change

Knowing that Cayce's life was beset by many adversities, misfortunes, and suffering, some may wonder why the contact alone with Archangel Michael wouldn't be enough to solve his problems. Questions were asked in a reading as to why he had to endure such adversity in his work, and the response clearly established the responsibilities that befell anyone who attempts to devote his or her life in service to others: "He that leads, or *would* direct, is continually beset by the forces that *would* undermine. He that endureth to the end shall wear the crown."[24]

Trials and tribulations are tests for souls on the earth, and Archangel Michael is a force that provides strength and faith in times of personal and planetary crisis. His role is not to remove the adversity, but, as in Cayce's case, so that the group members would hold fast to their ideals even though there would be storms of adversity and periods of darkness. Archangel Michael's message was that the work would succeed in bringing enlightenment to future generations, if they would but persevere. Hence, those "that endureth to the end shall wear the crown."

Adversity and darkness have been the pattern for many mystics, prophets, and sages. As a young girl, Joan of Arc made the pronouncement that she had spoken with Archangel Michael and that he had commanded that it was her duty to save France. Even during the periods of her trial, when she was harshly chastised for heresy, she fearlessly explained that she regularly spoke with angels. She said that the archangel Michael, in particular, had aided her in battle, encouraging her every step of the way. Physically, Joan of Arc did not survive her persecution by the church, yet she exuded no fear when she was sentenced to die or when she was burned at the stake. She would renounce none of the testimony of the angelic communion.

Jesus, in His great agony in the garden of Gethsemane, even though He had conscious communion with the angels, archangels, even the Father Himself, was beset by doubts and fear. Even He, the night before His crucifixion, felt the inescapable darkness before the dawn of resurrection: "My soul is exceeding sorrowful unto death ... " (Mark 14:34)

Even though we may go through the passage called "the dark night of the soul," there is a voice, a comfort, a *truth* which will sustain us in that dark night:

"MAKE KNOWN THAT LOVE, THAT GLORY, THAT POWER IN HIS NAME, THAT NONE BE AFRAID; FOR I,

MICHAEL, HAVE SPOKEN!"[25]

Each of us might take this message to heart. We take comfort that in our own spiritual journey, in our quest to understand our role in this coming divine age, the directions will be given. The messages of Archangel Michael are spoken to us, and they apply to us as individuals and to this world in transition, a world in its own garden of Gethsemane. The Cayce readings indicate that each person who is now on earth is here to potentially assist the earth in its spiritual transformation and evolution to higher consciousness. Not that the way will be easy, but all who seek to bring about this spiritual renaissance will indeed be shown the way, through dreams, intuition, meditation; some may even have the experience of direct communion with an angel, archangel, or the Master Himself. We should *expect* such reassurances.

"Every experience is an assurance," the sleeping Cayce said. "And as He has given, behold the face of the angel ever stands before the throne of God; the awareness in self that thou may be one with, equal with, the Father-God, as His child, as the brother of the Christ ... And as the awareness comes, it is as the angel of hope, the angel of announcing, the angel of declaiming, the angel that would warn, the angel that would protect. For, these are ever as awarenesses, as consciousnesses of the abiding presence of that 'He hath given his angels charge concerning thee' ... "[26]

As we hold to that belief, remembering that faith and desire create the world as we know it, then indeed will this become a reality. If we have the assurances of the archangels for us, what in this world could possibly be against us?

A final message from Archangel Michael, which was delivered to the Search for God Study Group in 1933:

"BOW THINE HEADS, O YE MEN THAT WOULD SEEK HIS PRESENCE! BE STRONG IN HIS MIGHT! FALTER

Divine Intervention

NOT AT THINE OWN WEAK SELF! KNOW THAT THY REDEEMER LIVETH … WILT THOU, THEN, O MAN, MAKE KNOWN THINE OWN DECISIONS? WILL YE BE ONE WITH HIM? THE WAY WHICH I GUARD LEADS TO THAT OF GLORY IN THE MIGHT OF THE LORD. I, MICHAEL, WOULD GUIDE THEE. DO NOT DISOBEY. DO NOT FALTER. THOU KNOWEST THE WAY."[27]

Chapter 4

Halaliel - Lord of the Hard Way

"He that leadeth into captivity shall go into captivity: he that killeth with the sword must be killed with the sword. Here is the patience and the faith of the saints." - Revelation 13:9-10

The Lord of Karma

ON only rare occasions, Cayce's readings came through with no particular voice identifying itself by name. There were, however, some exceptions. In chapter 2, for example, the story was shared of how Cayce's old friend Dr. Hill announced his presence during a reading. Also Archangel Michael spoke several times to the study group for whom Cayce had agreed to deliver the "work readings" as well as the weekly instructional readings for the group's study in spiritual development.

But, as we have seen, Michael spoke loudly and clearly to deliver some powerful messages that profoundly affected the group. With unmistakable energy, he reminded them of their highest spiritual ideals and even chastised them for straying and bickering among themselves.

It is generally believed that the source of the readings was the vast, universal unconscious mind which Cayce was able to tap every time he lay down to give a reading. It is also believed that the readings - and all the psychic work Cayce did in his lifetime - were guided by the Christ.

However, in the mid-1930s, as the study group members continued to collect the readings and prepare what would become the published volumes called *A Search for God,* they noticed another change of tone. Suddenly, Hugh Lynn Cayce, Gladys Davis, and other close friends of the Cayce family were greeted by a new archangel, one whose presence would create a division within the group.

"*Come*, my children! Ye no doubt have gained from the comment this day that a new initiate has spoken in or through this channel [Edgar Cayce]; Halaliel, that was with those in the beginning who warred with those that separated themselves and became as naught."[28]

Hugh Lynn remarked that this reading had a noticeable edge to it, an unusual commanding tone which indicated an apparent shift from the universal forces directing the information. This shift had a name as well: Halaliel. Gladys Davis and Gertrude Cayce also noticed the difference. It was a distinctive change in the *source* of the reading, and this made them uneasy.

Who was Halaliel?

This question was posed in a subsequent reading. Although the reply indicated that Halaliel was an angel from the higher spiritual kingdoms, the uneasiness was not dispelled.

"Who is Halaliel, the one who gave us a message on October 15th?" Mrs. Cayce asked.

"One in and with whose courts Ariel fought when there was the rebellion in heaven," Cayce said. "Where is Ariel, and who was he? A companion of Lucifer or Satan ... "[29] This indicates that Halaliel was an archangel on the side of Michael who fought against Satan before and during their fall from grace.

The "rebellion in heaven" is depicted in an interesting light in the Cayce readings. Long before our material universe came into being, all souls and archangels were companions of God, completely aware of their individuality, yet had communion with God. The souls and archangels had unlimited co-creative powers. Each was a miniature replica of God, containing all of God's abilities and potentialities. The "rebellion" was a spiritual diversion of consciousness contrary to God's creation. A sector of the archangels began to focus increasing energy into their own individual creations and diverse states of consciousness. Eventually, these angelic beings began to work in an opposite direction from God's divine design of the universe.

Legions of angels and archangels who were maintaining their conscious relationship with the Creator became aware that great numbers of their own were beginning to "forget" that they were at some former time one with God. They became enamored with their own powers and creations. When the archangels tried to bring the wayward souls back to remembrance of the original plan of God's creation, there was great resistance and discord.

As Thomas Sugrue wrote in the biography, *There Is a River - The Story of Edgar Cayce*: "Certain souls became bemused with their own power and began to experiment with it. They mingled with the dust of the stars and the winds of the spheres, feeling them, becoming part of them ... This was the fall in spirit, or the revolt of the angels."[30]

Halaliel is an archangel depicted as one of those who attempted to assist when this great dividing of the forces began. He and many other archangels - including Michael - became engaged in what may be called "the battle of remembrance versus forgetfulness." They were fighting for the souls who were going deeper and deeper into selfishness. Lucifer and Ariel, once great archangels in the realm of God, became leaders for the side of the angels and souls who desired to go their own way, irrespective of God's desires. Thus, the good and evil (remembrance and forgetfulness) became living states of consciousness, now represented by Light and Darkness. Today, eons of time later, this battle is waged in the earthly realm within the souls of humanity, as we daily confront the choice to be selfless or selfish.

A Cayce reading confirms Halaliel's role with the archangels:

"Halaliel is the one who from the beginning has been a leader of the heavenly host, who has defied Ariel, who has *made the ways that have been heavy* - but as the means for UNDERSTANDING."[31] (Author's italics)

From the above reading, it is obvious that Halaliel's role in the spiritual hierarchy is substantial. The term "heavenly host" refers to the angels of heaven as a whole. The problem, however, with the influence of Halaliel as one of these ministering archangels is his *approach* to humankind as a divine helper. The reference to Halaliel making "the ways that have been heavy" concerned those who were receiving the psychic readings from Cayce. Would they find themselves under the direction of a difficult taskmaster? As there are a variety of religious philosophies in the earth and many different ways and approaches to understanding God, the archangels also direct humanity in their own unique way. What was meant by "ways that have been heavy"?

This brings into light the law of *karma* - the law of cause and effect. Karma in Sanskrit means "act" or "deed." It is the law by which every action, thought, word, or deed creates an equal reaction of equivalent force that returns to us. Cayce would sometimes counsel people who were encountering the "return" of their deeds and, in effect, was saying, "Your chickens have come home to roost!" The return of deeds, thoughts, etc., occurs under the law of karma.

Dr. Richard H. Drummond, a world-renowned theologian, drew from biblical examples of karma in his book *A Life of Jesus the Christ*: " ... along with many, many quotations or rephrasings of 'Whatever a man sows, that he will also reap' (Galatians 6:7), there are frequent references to Jesus' teaching 'with what measure ye mete, it is measured to thee again' ... karma ... is indeed seen in the Cayce readings as a divine, cosmic principle."[32]

In other words, everything we do returns to us in the same spirit in which it was carried out. The Bible describes karma in the Book of Revelation 13:10, "He that leadeth into captivity shall go into captivity: he that killeth with the sword must be killed with the sword. Here is the patience and the faith of the saints."

However, to correctly understand the law, one must also understand how it works with the concept of reincarnation. Reincarnation is the concept that the soul - an individual's consciousness - does not die when the body dies, that it continues on in another dimension and can seek another body into which to be born. There are principally two reasons why a soul returns in a new embodiment: by choice and by necessity. In either case, the soul chooses its parents and, therefore, the circumstances which will give it the best opportunity for growth and to make reparations for its accumulated karma.

Reincarnation has been termed the "cycle of necessity." In Sanskrit it is called *samsara* or "running together." A goal in certain branches of Buddhism is to correct all karma and escape samsara, thereby attaining *nirvana* or heaven. It is this cycle of necessity - as humans continue to create karma through desires contrary to the design of God's pattern of a harmonious universe - that was meant by Halaliel representing "the ways that have been heavy." The story of the soul's karma through the earth will be explored in depth in chapter 7.

The archangels - Michael, Raphael, Gabriel, Uriel as well as Halaliel - have, since the beginning of the fall of spirit, continued to try to bring back to souls the remembrance of their divine origin, their oneness with God. Although messengers of God, these archangels each have a unique role in the earth's spiritual evolvement. As Archangel Michael is "Lord of the Way which leads to Christ," Uriel is the archangel of salvation or one who awakens the sleeping mortals to higher spiritual knowledge, "saving" souls from the purely materialistic consciousness. Archangel Raphael presides over the forces of spiritual and physical healing in the earth. Archangel Gabriel, who announced to the Virgin Mary that she was to give birth to the Messiah, is the angel of annunciation, resurrection, mercy, and revelation. According to Dionysius in his *Mystical Theology and the Celestial Hierarchy*, all archangels "are the messengers bearing divine decrees."[33]

Halaliel has his decrees to carry out, but his function is as the Lord of Karma, a guiding consciousness that governs the law of cause and effect. Through this law, human beings bring themselves, eventually, to conscious remembrance of God under his dominion through "heavy" trials. This cycle which Halaliel governs, in which we "pay as we go" in life - and in life after life - is actually a practical and merciful mechanism by which we can learn by our mistakes, rather than continue to make mistakes unchecked.

Archangels as Laws of the Universe

In a large scope, each archangel represents a state of consciousness, an attitude, an inspiration. What we experience in spiritual consciousness in the material realm is a reflection of the *source* of a particular consciousness in the spiritual realms. These sources are the archangels - the orderly facets of the hierarchy of God. The Cayce readings indicate that the universal laws themselves are ensouled by archangels. For example, the laws of enlightenment, wisdom, transformation, cause and effect are divine *consciousnesses*. The question was posed to Cayce in a reading, "Are angels and archangels synonymous with that which we call the laws of the universe?" Cayce replied, "They are as the laws of the universe; as is Michael the Lord of the Way, *not* the Way but the Lord of the Way ... "[34]

This means that when people are in complete harmony with their spiritual ideal - or their spiritual purpose in life - they are complying with the universal law of love. Then Michael makes the way open so that they can be awakened to even greater spiritual awareness. In the after-death state of consciousness, Dr. Rodonaia was in harmony with the law (archangel) of Wisdom; he naturally gravitated to that consciousness. Likewise, Halaliel is the governing angel of the law of karma, cause and effect. He is a leading angel whose influence leads to spiritual growth, but that growth is gained on a path and through trials which are - as Cayce said - "heavy."

When Halaliel's presence became evident through the readings, Hugh Lynn was adamant that the group should not blindly settle for some entity, even if the information came from an archangel. Hugh Lynn felt that Halaliel was now interfering with the spiritual lessons, the Search for God work. Several of Cayce's associates disagreed, arguing that the archangel Michael had given inspiring instructions, but they should follow the advice of Halaliel, too.

"Though Edgar Cayce still maintained his voice and his manner, inflection, etc.," Hugh Lynn wrote later, "the statement was made that a character known as Halaliel could direct the material to be given in the readings in a clearer more organized fashion. It was indicated that a decision needed to be made as to whether this offer of clarification could be accepted by the group."[35] All except two members of Cayce's group wanted to reject the directions of Halaliel. "It was for all a period of questioning, testing, and decision making," Hugh Lynn said.

The group became divided and sought more information about Halaliel through the readings. A cryptic passage indicated the continued influence of Halaliel, but placed the responsibility of this teacher's appearance on the *group members themselves*. Cayce said:

" ... for, as will be seen, my children, there has been appointed one that may aid thee in thy future lessons, and he will be thy teacher, thy guide, one sent through the power of thine own desires ... Not the Christ, but His messenger, with the Christ from the beginning, and is to other worlds what the Christ is to this earth."[36]

The Christ Consciousness vs. Halaliel

Hugh Lynn was disturbed that the reading indicated the information was being directed by "Not the Christ, but His messenger." He had always felt that his father's readings were directed from the universal forces, and it was the group's duty to abide by that high ideal.

Part of that ideal meant refusing direction from any source but the Christ Consciousness. Hugh Lynn was suspect as to whether Halaliel came to intervene or interfere with the group: If he was to other worlds what Christ is to this one, what was he doing *here*? Why should he want to influence the study group members in their work? These were questions which set uneasily with Edgar Cayce, his wife, his secretary, and his son. As we've seen, Cayce was often wary about the nature of the readings; he worried about how "open" he was to outside influences during his trance states. He rarely acknowledged even the archangel Michael, but instead viewed that God had sent a messenger. God should be the focus, Cayce said, not the messenger. Halaliel, however, was acting in a larger capacity than a mere messenger in Cayce's work - he wanted to *direct* the readings.

Hugh Lynn, Gladys Davis, and Gertrude Cayce couldn't accurately explain what made them feel a slight foreboding when they considered Halaliel and his influence in the readings. Yet they knew they had the power to choose or reject Halaliel as a teacher. The reading placed the responsibility with the group: "Thine own selves, then, may prevent his [Halaliel] being, meeting, living, dwelling, with thee."[37]

The particular study group reading in which this message came through had a tone which was uncharacteristically aggressive. Halaliel seemed to be giving the group a sort of spiritual ultimatum: "Accept, then, that presented here, and arrange same; for thine presentations must, from here, take a turn ... Accept ye?"[38] No one in the group responded to Halaliel's request. If anything, they were shocked by the drastic change in the usually patient progression of the reading through Cayce. The energy within the room was odd; charged, full - as if a spiritual pressure was being placed upon all present. Gertrude Cayce continued to conduct the reading, and the other members present bowed their heads in prayer. Halaliel, obviously impatient with the group's indecision, reprimanded them in the midst of the reading:

"*PAY ATTENTION TO WHAT YOU ARE DOING HERE!*"

Several of the group members felt that this message was directed at them, including Gertrude Cayce and Gladys Davis. The energy in the room was very chaotic and discordant. Why this intrusion? Was it that a matter of harsh times requires a harsh teacher? Was there an internal battle of the light versus the darkness taking place within the individuals of the study group? Had the group gone astray in its studies or application of the spiritual truths? Had the Universal Forces

Halaliel - Lord of the Hard Way

sent Halaliel to assist them in their group work? Such were the questions, discussions, and debates among the members. Bitter arguments ensued by the few who wanted Halaliel's guidance, and some relationships were tense at best within the group.

Cayce's health was in a particularly sensitive state at the time - he hadn't been feeling physically well for weeks. A few members of the group were dealing with karmic issues of their own: resentment, self-condemnation, being overly critical and jealous. Above all else, they were human beings, subject to periods of weakness as everyone else. However, because of the intensity of the spiritual lessons and their meditation and prayer as a group together, there was a magnification of energy among the relationships of the group members. Their spiritual abilities were awakening and dissension became no small issue.

Everything was magnified - good and bad. They were - individually and as a group - obviously passing through a period of karmic testing. They had reached a place where their spiritual knowledge had to be applied through this period of trial. It wasn't easy on any of them. The timing of Halaliel's entrance as a karmic teacher and the group's unsettling experiences are particularly synchronistic. Clearly, they were on the right path, they had the guidance of the Most High, and yet they had to make a choice between receiving guidance from the Lord of Karma or from the Christ Consciousness.

A reading was given by Cayce, separate from the *Search for God* work, and a question was asked about following the advice of messengers, archangels, and spirit guides.

"This - this - *this*, my friends, even but limits," the reading said; "while in Him is the Whole. Would thou make of thyself, of thyselves, a limited means of activity? Would thou seek to be hindered by those things that have made of many contending forces that continue to war one with another even in the air, even in the elemental forces?"[39] Another reading in that same series stated: "Let *Him* send whom *He* would for the development, but rather prepare thine own body, thine own soul, for that meeting with Him."[40]

These readings indicated to the group that it was, in many ways, settling for less if the members accepted the teacher Halaliel to direct them. To limit themselves to the guidance of Halaliel, therefore, would hinder the group from its goal of reaching the ultimate spiritual attainment: the Christ Consciousness.

This path would help them transcend the cycle of necessity, their karma, through prayer, meditation, and applying the spiritual disciplines given to them in the Search for God material. Why would they willingly step back into the path of trial and error from which they'd come? To accept Halaliel as *the source* for the spiritual lessons would have placed them in that realm of hard experience.

Other Perspectives

W. H. Church, a Cayce historian and expert on the readings, had an interesting viewpoint about Halaliel and his influence on the study group. "Halaliel, appearing to the group when he did, could have acted at the Master's direction, precisely because they were then going through a karmic phase that called for a hard taskmaster - unless it could be otherwise met ... if Halaliel had been sent to them through the power of their own desires - whether conscious or otherwise - was that good or bad? For each of them knew his or her own spiritual shortcomings, and one or two of them may have trembled. Secondly, if Halaliel was to other worlds what the Christ is to this one, as had been stated, had he not his own sheep to tend to? What was he doing in the Christ's domain at this time? Did it bode well or ill? Doubts must have occurred to them on this score."[41]

Meanwhile, as the readings continued, the unease never quite left Hugh Lynn. He was very worried that the group members had conjured up a messenger whose influence would be more of a hindrance than anything else to his father's work.

"I was concerned," Hugh Lynn explained. "My father was not, for

Halaliel - Lord of the Hard Way

all intents and purposes, a medium. True, when the attunement was right, there was an angelic message, a voice, a divine proclamation. This, however, was the exception rather than the rule. Dad did not ever consider himself to be a medium for the spirit world. He personally told the group to focus their ideals and desires on the Master - and let Him direct how He would. But there were times when Dad would say, 'If people want the information in the readings to come from Uncle Joe who was on the other side, that's where they'd get it from. If they wanted the reading to come from a divine messenger, they'd get that, too.' It really depended upon the *desires* of the person requesting the reading."

Halaliel also came up in the psychic readings of famed medium Eileen Garrett. Her spirit guide, according to Cayce's reading for her, relied upon information given through the archangel Halaliel.

"On one occasion," Hugh Lynn recounted, "following a reading with Eileen Garrett, her control [spirit guide], Uvani, offered to clarify the readings, and a question was asked in a reading as to whether this would be a wise idea or not ... I think this is a similar kind of diversion brought on by the stress and trial through which the whole group, as well as the nation, was passing and because of the physical disturbances Edgar Cayce suffered at the time."[42] This occurred when there was great economic difficulty in the so-called Depression years, and also during this time Cayce experienced a period of ill health.

The reading Hugh Lynn referred to is one of the "work readings," where the question was posed to Cayce, "Would it be advisable for Edgar Cayce to follow her [Eileen Garrett's] suggestions as to seeking assistance from the entity described [Halaliel] whom Uvani claims will increase the coherence and power of the readings?"

The answer was short and to the point: "Does Uvani claim to know better than the Master who made him?"[43] It was clearly indicated that Cayce's group should not accept the ongoing influence of any force other than the Christ's. However, the archangel Michael's messages in the readings were in keeping with the highest spiritual ideals because he was directing attention to the greater reality and ultimate manifestation of the Christ Consciousness.

Still, more readings began to reflect the tone and consciousness of Halaliel. A series of readings in the mid-1930s were taken on the state of world affairs and on future events. Generally, these readings would seldom predict specific events, but would only give current conditions and advice on how things could be bettered. An ominous tone, however, to several of the world affairs readings have led some to believe they were given by Halaliel. Clearly, the aggressive tone is very different from the rest of the collection of Cayce readings which rarely reflect a type of personality of any kind:

"The earth will be broken up in the western portion of America. The greater portion of Japan must go into the sea. The upper portion of Europe will be changed as in the twinkling of an eye. Land will appear off the east coast of America. There will be the upheavals in the Arctic and in the Antarctic that will make for the eruption of volcanoes in the Torrid areas, and there will be shifting then of the poles ... "[44]

Specific global events of such magnitude were made by Cayce on a few rare occasions. Some students of the readings will dispute these earth changes accounts, saying that the information came from Halaliel who prophesied only catastrophic ends. Others say that Halaliel was one who came to warn as the Lord of Karma, to allow people to prepare for the great upheavals imminent at the end of this century.

Still, in this same world affairs reading, there is an interesting passage which seems to indicate that there is indeed a form of battle ensuing as the days of the old millennium come to a close:

"For with the great numbers of the gathering of the hosts of those that have hindered and would make for man and his weaknesses stumbling blocks, they shall wage war with the spirits of light that come into the earth for this awakening; that have been and are being called by those of the sons of men into the service of the living God."[45]

Halaliel, then, may be seen as one who will be a warrior for the Light during this time. But how will he reign? The key word here in this passage is *awakening*. This is at the heart of the call and influence of the angelic realms. We are on the verge of great changes, crises, and the probability of universal spiritual enlightenment. As we take stock of ourselves and our world, we can clearly see that there are great conflicts arising not only on the world's stage but within ourselves; perspectives, beliefs, the way we live and do what we do. How will we fare in these days of intense transition?

As was true with the Search for God group, it will depend largely on our spiritual state of being, our attitudes and beliefs. Again, the power of thought and desire and our personal actions bring the world as we know it into being. What do we expect and what are we building for ourselves? Perhaps Halaliel has come into our time as one who proclaims a "reckoning"; that there will be a period of time where great darkness shall precede the great enlightenment. This seems to be the pattern for all: In order to fully comprehend the Light, we must first pass through and understand the darkness.

To examine both sides of the Halaliel controversy, it is important to consider whether he came to warn and advise or interfere with his karmic activity. Clearly, Halaliel was taking to task not just the individuals in the study group, but all of us who are on a spiritual quest. Great lessons are upon us, and it is up to us how we learn them. We can learn through rigid cause-and-effect circumstances or through the grace of acceptance of all aspects of our lives. Halaliel's intervention brought dissension to the group members. But his question is relevant: *Whom do you wish to serve? Choose ye.* There is the same admonition in the Old Testament's Book of Deuteronomy which says: "I have set before thee this day life and good, and death and evil … " (30:15) This choice is being set before us as individuals, groups, and nations. We might ask questions of our own lives in transition: *What am I here to do? What role do I have in the new millennium?* The basic premise for leading a full spiritual life is embodied in a very simple passage in the readings: "Forgive, if ye would be forgiven. *That* is knowledge. Be friendly, if ye would have friends. *That* is knowledge. Be lovely, if ye would have the love even of thy Father; for He is love."[46]

These simple truths are made into ultimate challenges for us in these days. The choice of how difficult or how easy learning these lessons will be is strictly up to us. Learning spiritual lessons under the direction of Halaliel and the direction of Christ may be two separate paths which lead to the same Source. One, Halaliel, represents the karmic path, the warring consciousness, the battle and struggle to reach the light, and the law of cause and effect. While this at times has its place, the Christ's way, on the other hand, is representative of accepting the circumstances of our lives in patience, love, joy, forbearance, and forgiveness; and ultimately following Him to the ascension. This path is the most direct way to work toward divine fulfillment and awakening.

Halaliel and the Christ represent two approaches to spiritual development: under Christ's direction, we learn the lesson of patience through daily living: our intimate relationships, friends, families, day-to-day experiences. Under Halaliel's direction, we learn patience through the sorrow, pain, and suffering we create for ourselves through folly. Patience is ultimately learned in both instances, but the *approach* to this facet of spirituality is different. It is the *way* in which we choose to learn our spiritual lessons that calls upon different teachers. In the end, however, we learn from both levels of experience: Pain and sorrow, and joy and happiness can lead to soul development. It might be said that Christ completes the soul development where Halaliel begins. In other words, grace surpasses and overcomes karma. In this light, Halaliel is a valid and important teacher. We endure "crucifixion" under the law of karma (Halaliel); but we are redeemed through "resurrection" under the law of grace (Christ).

With the exception of two people, as mentioned earlier, the Search for God study group rejected Halaliel as a director of its spiritual lessons. Speaking once again from the level of the universal mind, a subsequent reading seemed to reprimand the group for drawing Halaliel's influence into this realm: "And ye in thy blindness, thy foolishness, thy *desire* for self, look for some *easy* way; when all the ease, all the hope, all the life there is *is* in Him!"[47]

Two members of the study group left to pursue other spiritual interests, feeling that the Search for God group had made a mistake in rejecting the offer of Halaliel's guidance. Yet, the remaining group members received a message which seemed to indicate that while God will send His messengers, they should never become preoccupied with a specific teacher when they could receive guidance from the Teacher of teachers:

"Let not thy heart be troubled. Ye believe in God. Believe also in Him, who hath given, 'Lo, I am with thee always, even unto the end of the world.' Though there may come disturbances and turmoils, know that peace cometh only in Him - and in doing that thou knowest *to* do."[48]

Chapter 5

God's Diversity: The Wisdom of the Angels

"Thus, while the Celestial Hierarchies are the transmitters of Providential Life to all below them, they constitute for the aspiring soul which unites itself to them a spiritual ladder of ascent from Earth to Heaven ... which is the Unitive Way whereby men may attain to true friendship with God ... " - Dionysius the Areopagite

The Angelic Hierarchy

RUDOLF Steiner believed that all material life emanates from spiritual states of consciousness which interpenetrate as well as exist outside our three-dimensional world. He was gifted with the clairvoyant ability to perceive the higher, spiritual dimensions and celestial realms of the angels and archangels. These realms remain greatly unnoticed by most of us, except when we sleep and enter the higher dimensions through dreaming or enter into deep states of meditation. Everything in our earth realm is governed by a source of intelligence which resides somewhere in the orders of the divine hierarchy. The Cayce readings often said that all things in the earth are a mere shadow of what exists in the spiritual realms. In other words, we only have a physical reflection on earth of realities which reside in the spiritual world. For example, when Dr. Rodonaia had his three-day death experience, he went to the source of divine wisdom, which he perceived as a "sphere of intelligence," a being or archangel. As a philosopher during much of his professional life, Dr. Rodonaia had studied the concept of wisdom, but in the higher worlds he experienced Wisdom as the archangel, the source from which wisdom emanates.

"Here on earth we say, 'wisdom,' and say it is a higher attribute of attained knowledge. Here it is an idea," Dr. Rodonaia said. "In the spiritual world Wisdom is a *thousand worlds*."

Dr. Rodonaia has tried, with a great deal of frustration, to translate his trek to the "beloved realm of Sophia" (Wisdom) to his congregations and listening audiences. Some experiences, however, are not easily described in words in our three-dimensional world. Dr. Rodonaia's transformative experience with Wisdom as a loving divine intelligence during his death experience was very similar to that of Emanuel Swedenborg, the Swedish mystic-clairvoyant, mathematician, physicist, and biologist, who believed that the highest purpose for souls is to achieve union with God through love and wisdom. Swedenborg was able to peer into the angelic kingdoms through deep meditation and retain an almost photographic memory of the realms of the angels. He wrote detailed descriptions of the angels and their realms of abode in *Heaven and Hell*. Swedenborg confirms Cayce's view that all which is on earth is a mere shadow of what exists in the spirit world: He states that angelic wisdom greatly exceeds human wisdom and that all things which the angels perceive exceed earthly things, because it corresponds to their wisdom.

"The wisdom of the angels is indescribable in words; it can only be illustrated by some general things. Angels can express in a single word what a man cannot express in a thousand words. Again, a single angelic word contains innumerable things that cannot be expressed in the words of human language; for in each of the things uttered by angels there are arcana of wisdom in continuous connection that human knowledges never reach."[49]

Swedenborg believed that just as our physical world is arranged and ordered in branches of society, classes, and organizations, the angelic worlds also function in a Divine Order. Paola Giovetti, paraphrasing Swedenborg, wrote on the order of angels:

" ... the societies of angels in heaven are distinguished by their

God's Diversity: The Wisdom of the Angels

activities and customs. There are some societies that take care of the little children; others teach them when they grow up; others foster the simple and good in the Christian world and lead them toward Heaven … All these functions are functions of the Lord performed by the angels, because the angels perform them not for themselves, but on the basis of the divine order."[50]

The Cayce readings indicated that the hosts of angels are not only mindful of humanity's development through the material world, but it is their greater mission to quicken us to the awareness of God. As the archangels are considered to be the voices of God, the multitude of groupings of the angels act as the *senses* of God. These branches are the many levels and many diverse spiritual and material expressions which God has for experiencing Himself in individualized entities, spirits, and levels of consciousness.

The souls of all people on earth are like the leaves of a large tree; the angels and archangels are the branches; the entire tree is God. Humanity is considered one of the highest branches of God's creation: We embody all that make up the lower, physical kingdoms of the earth, and we also possess all aspects of the higher spiritual kingdoms. The entire pattern of the "tree" is imprinted within each "leaf." Much in the same way we have different levels of consciousness of the body, the "physical hierarchies" of atoms, cells, and corpuscles; these build into the larger systems of organs in our bodies, which in turn make up the "whole" person. The angels, archangels, and souls represent individuations of "the whole" of God. The Cayce readings say that each soul is a corpuscle[51] in the body of God. To reveal fully the vastness of this picture, a reading also said that the earth is an atom in a universe of worlds! In the earth's collective consciousness of all humanity, we make up only a small - but important - portion of the totality of God, yet that small part contains the pattern for the whole. The microcosm is a miniature replica of the macrocosm.

The Angelic Hierarchy - Divine Branches of God

Hierarchy is defined as any arrangement of principles or things in an ascending or descending order. One way we may understand how the angelic hierarchy operates is to look at the various levels of an institution, such as a hospital. On the first level, we have the emergency room, which helps people in immediate critical need. This level could correspond with the guardian angels who appear in our lives at times of crisis or emergency. At the next level we have the entire staff of the hospital physicians who work in countless capacities to help us get well: the general practitioners. Next there are the surgeons, who are "higher" in the hierarchy because their skills are more specialized than a general practitioner physician. These can be seen as guardians of the groups of patients in the hospital, overseeing the work of the lower levels. Then there are the counselors, psychiatrists, and ministers who are responsible for the mental and spiritual welfare of the hospital's patients and their families. These are the ministering angels.

Overseeing the entire operation is the medical board of directors, which represents the archangels, who dictate policy and law throughout the whole hierarchy. Within this intricate conglomeration is the orderly operating of one institution. They all work separately, yet the organization serves one purpose: to help heal. This is the same as the celestial hierarchy, with each force or law of the universe governing one particular aspect of helping humanity and manifesting innumerable facets of God.

Although it would be seemingly impossible to identify and name the order of angelic realms, a certain Christian mystic, Pseudo-Dionysius the Areopagite, who lived in the fifth century A.D., learned through visions and meditation the orders of the angel kingdoms. His writings include *The Celestial Hierarchy* and *The Ecclesiastical Hierarchy* and other works dealing with the orders of angelic beings.

God's Diversity: The Wisdom of the Angels

The Celestial Hierarchy depicts the material world as a single physical emblem of the larger, divine reality. In his works, Pseudo-Dionysius outlined the nine orders of the hierarchy which have been widely accepted by Christian theologians since the Middle Ages. (See Figure 1.) The nine orders of the celestial hierarchy are as follows: Seraphim, Cherubim, Thrones, Dominions, Virtues, Powers, Principalities, Archangels, Angels. The treatment of these branches in this particular chapter will attempt to detail how each level of the celestial orders influences us in our lives.

The Supreme Hierarchy: Seraphim, Cherubim, Thrones

The Seraphim represent the highest order, the angels of love, light, and fire. Their name originates from the Hebrew word, *seraphs*, meaning "love." The mystical significance of fire is cleansing. It is a symbol of purification, according to the Edgar Cayce readings. The biblical verse which states, that all shall "be tried with fire" (I Peter 1:7) means that all will be cleansed and purified from any earthly distraction which stands in the way of spiritual awakening. More fundamentalist teachings view this verse in a negative light, as the fires of hell and damnation. Yet, if we consider fire as a purifying factor, then the Seraphim burn away all that is not in accordance with our highest spiritual ideals.

This is particularly evident in the Book of Isaiah, for when the prophet sees the Seraphim, he proclaims, "Woe is me! for I am undone; because I am a man of unclean lips ... " (6:5)

At this point an angel of the Seraphim places a burning coal upon the lips of Isaiah and says, "Lo, this hath touched thy lips; and thine iniquity is taken away, and thy sin purged." (6:7) Fire, in this case, is a purifying activity, not a destructive force.

The Angelic Hierarchy

Supreme Hierarchy	**Seraphim** **Cherubim** **Thrones**
Middle Hierarchy	**Dominions** **Virtues** **Powers**
Lower Hierarchy	**Principalities** **Archangels** **Angels**

Figure 1.
The Angelic Hierarchy
According to Pseudo-Dionysius the Areopagite

The angels of Seraphim are always surrounding the Godhead or the center from which all life flows out to consciousness and creation. The Seraphim also are depicted as one of the main "choirs" of angels, which emanate from what the Cayce readings called "the music of the spheres." When Jesus was born, the celestial music was praise from the Seraphim, which was powerful enough to have literally been heard on earth, as was detailed in the Gospel of Luke: "And suddenly there was with the angel a multitude of the heavenly host praising God, and saying, Glory to God in the highest, and on earth peace, good will toward men." (2:13-14)

Many people who have returned from near-death experiences have mentioned hearing indescribably beautiful music in the dark tunnel which leads them to the Light. People have reported the music as not merely sound, but it seemed to be divine living emanations from the Light. This phenomenon correlates to the Seraphim being the angels of light and love. One individual said that this music of the spheres appeared to be "the musical symphony of God." No doubt, the celestial music came from the realm of the holy choir of the Seraphim. In many religious rites and ceremonies, the use of chanting and music is vital to the process of prayer and meditation as a means of attunement to God.

The Cherubim is the second highest order of angels. Translated from Assyrian, Cherubim means "one who prays" or "one who intercedes." The prophet Ezekiel had a profound vision of the Cherubim. Chapter 10 of the Book of Ezekiel seemed to foretell the coming of the Messiah. In his vision, a man enters among the angels which comprise the Cherubim, withdraws coals (which indicates the Seraphim), and scatters them over the city. Jesus has been called the Divine Intercessor, and in Ezekiel's vision this intercessor is going out from the heavenly host to bring intercession and cleansing (fire) for humanity.

The Cherubim also serve as the memory of God or the angels who guard celestial records of knowledge. It is interesting to note that Jesus, as the Divine Intercessor between God and humanity, said during His ministry that "the Comforter ... whom the Father will send in my name, he shall ... bring all things to your remembrance ... " (John 14:26) This fulfills the vision of Ezekiel as well as fulfills the role of the Cherubim as the "knowledge-givers."

When Edgar Cayce gave a past-life reading for an individual, he would read from the akashic records or the "Book of God's Remembrance." Often during these readings, he would have a vision of encountering the "keeper of the records," who always handed him the book of the person for whom the reading was intended.

Flower Newhouse, one of the early angelologists of this century and - according to the Cayce readings - one of the best authorities on angels because of her clairvoyant abilities, said that the Cherubim contemplate the Wisdom of God and emanate that Wisdom. It is particularly interesting to note that in Dr. Rodonaia's three-day death experience, he felt and knew that "Wisdom" was a living, divine being of God, not merely a thought form or state of consciousness. It seems reasonable to state that Dr. Rodonaia dwelt in the realm of the Cherubim during his death experience and then returned to earth to impart that wisdom as part of his ministry.

The Garden of Eden also was under the influence of the Cherubim, for these angelic beings guarded the tree of knowledge of good and evil. When we seek for inner spiritual guidance, the knowledge we receive in inspiration and revelation comes from the Cherubim branch of the angelic kingdom. The opposite extreme exists in the realm of Satan, the fallen archangel who was originally of the leader of the Cherubim. The serpent imparted the knowledge of good and evil to Adam and Eve in the Garden. Satan today is considered to be the governor of evil knowledge used for selfish purpose and gain. We will discuss Satan more fully in chapter 6.

The next angelic order is the Thrones. They govern God's justice. The Thrones are a source of the karmic forces, perhaps where the archangel Halaliel holds his position in the divine order. Dionysius says that through the Thrones God brings His justice to bear upon us. According to Jewish legend, many of the angels of this realm became numbered among the fallen angels and no longer occupy a position in the higher celestial hierarchy. The activities of the fallen angels of Thrones embody all activities of *injustice* or discord in the affairs of humanity in the earth. Although there always appears to be the ongoing battle of justice with injustice, it seems that eventually good will prevail over evil, and God's justice (grace) will overcome all opposing forces (karma). On the virtuous activities of the Thrones, however, Paola Giovetti writes:

"As for the Thrones, these were very lofty and sublime spirits and their name tells us that they transcend in purity every vile inclination, ascending toward the summit in a manner that is extraterrestrial. They withdraw steadfastly from every lowly action, seated as they are firmly and legitimately around Him who is indeed the Most High, gleaning what descends from the Divine principle."[52]

The Thrones also create the powerful spiritual impulse within the souls of humanity to "return home" in consciousness, to remember and return to God. They send out a powerful force of attraction, which eventually will lead all souls - regardless of their present state of consciousness - back to their divine heritage.

The Middle Hierarchy: Dominions, Virtues, Powers

Dominions or Dominations, the next level of the celestial hierarchy, manifest in the world as the forces of nature in all of its diversity and splendor - in the earthly animal, vegetable, and mineral kingdoms. The Cayce readings often indicated that one who understands nature walks close with God. For the majesty of the forests on earth reflect the glory of the divine order of the Dominions. Along these lines, the potential perfect plan and design of evolution inherent in all physical manifestation of the earth originate from the Dominions. The law of evolution in the spiritual realm of Dominions provides the pattern for all things to have individual consciousness and yet contain the pattern of universal oneness. This branch of the hierarchy can be seen as the originating source and eventual perfection of God's plan for creation.

Virtues are the angelic forces which manifest miracles in spirit and upon the earth. Whereas the Thrones emanate justice, Virtues emanate grace. According to the Cayce readings, when Jesus overcame the temptations during His forty days in the wilderness, He appropriately met and overcame the law of karma and was then freed and became the embodiment of the law of grace. Although there were many developments toward the state of grace by many masters and teachers, Jesus is believed to be the first human being to have fully attained that state of perfection (grace) in body, mind, and spirit. This concept seems to be in keeping with that presented in Jean Danielou's work,

The Angels and Their Mission, in which two angels of the Virtues escorted Christ's ascension forty days after His resurrection. The law of karma is life and death; the law of grace is eternal life without having the transition through the death experience. This grace epitomizes the majesty of the forces of the Virtues. The early Christians believed that when Jesus performed miracles, He called upon the angelic forces of the Virtues.

The third group of angelic influences in the middle hierarchy are the Powers, which are the warrior angelic intelligences believed to keep the demons and fallen angels at bay not only in the spiritual realms, but on earth. On the virtuous side, these angelic beings emanate creative power to the souls of humanity. According to Gustav Davidson's *Dictionary of Angels,* the Powers regulate punitive power, mercy, legislation, and sovereign power. In the rare cases of exorcism (which the Catholic church reluctantly admits is still practiced within the U.S.), the priest calls upon the presence of Christ to expel the demon, and the forces rallied emanate from the guardians of the Powers, who reign sovereign over demonic forces. The Cayce readings say that the very name of Jesus Christ *is* a vibrational power capable of dispelling any negative spirit, influence, or force.

Commanding the name will bring divine protection and intervention. Any form of power in the earth realm emanates from this branch of the divine hierarchy. At the height of its Source, the Powers are pure benevolent forces, yet they at times can be distorted for evil according to human will. Because the Powers are companionate rulers of cause and effect with the Thrones, the abuse or misuse of their pure energy will always call into play the role of the Thrones, who will return the activity of misuse to the sender, a situation which brings into play the karmic forces: " ... for whatsoever a man soweth, that shall he also reap." (Galatians 6:7) Flower Newhouse believed that under the authority of the Powers the angels of birth and death carry out God's justice.

The Lower Hierarchy: Principalities, Archangels, Angels

The Principalities (or Princedoms) are the highest angelic beings in the third triad of the angelic hierarchy. The diversity of the world's religions originates from these celestial intelligences. The leaders of nations have the capacity to be influenced by the Principalities - that is, if they will listen - and are provided with divine guidance in their decision making. As each person has an individual destiny to carry out, each collective nation also has a single destiny as well. In the same way that an organ of the body is made up of millions of cells which comprise the whole organ, each person in a nation is like a cell. When all people cooperate in a state of divinity, then the nation will be fully operative as an "organ" in the body of the One Force or God. The Principalities might be seen as the "nerve center" portion of the brain which governs the spiritual awakening of the masses. Flower Newhouse said that these angelic forces do not intervene nor guard "the policies of a nation, only its humanitarian incentives and its unique culture."[53]

It is one of the roles of the Archangels, the next order of the angelic hierarchy, to oversee the activities of the nations. At different periods of history various reigning Archangels divinely inspired our world through art, literature, music, religion, and mysticism. Although Archangels appear in the lower ranks of the celestial hierarchy, they seem to be able to command all the divine forces in carrying out their work, appearing on earth with the messages of the Most High, drawing upon the Thrones, Principalities, and Virtues. The higher named orders seem to be the *sources* from which they draw their activity. The rank to which Michael belongs, for example, may indeed be of the higher order *in activity*; as if in their very movement in consciousness, the Principalities, Virtues, and Thrones become the Archangels.

This operates much in the same way the Cayce readings say that Christ is the God-force *in activity*. It is the movement which determines the different activities of the One Force. In her book, *Rediscovering the Angels*, Flower Newhouse writes that the Archangels could evolve to the higher orders of the angelic hierarchy and remain there, but instead have chosen to help the souls of humanity remember their divine heritage: "Archangels possess tremendous development and could be in the ranks of any of the described Advanced Orders [celestial hierarchy], but they choose to be interpreters between the Higher Orders and the Ranks of Angels and men."[54] They have chosen to assist souls on earth reach their spiritual potential.

According to Rudolf Steiner, Michael is the leading Archangel who will guide the spiritual development of nations for the next several hundred years. His responsibility lies in bringing souls to full awakening of the Christ Consciousness at the conscious-mind level. He is also a representative of the Powers - which is why he is often depicted in art as the sword-bearer assisting individuals or groups to overcome darkness and evil influences.

According to *The Book of Enoch*, the seven leading Archangels are Uriel, Raphael, Raguel, Michael, Sarakiel, Gabriel, and Remiel. Each one in the third order of the celestial hierarchy has a unique role to play in the activities of all souls on earth. Archangel Uriel is believed to be the great alchemist who transforms misfortune and tribulation on earth into great advantages. A person might, for example, be fired from a job which had been his or her lifeblood for many years. Just as that individual thought that he or she was without hope, a much better position in a more successful company opens up and the person is hired. Afterward, much in awe of the good fortune, the individual realizes that out of the curse came a great blessing. Perhaps it is from the angelic realm of Uriel that we learn that when God closes the door in one area of our lives, He opens a window somewhere else. When we awaken a sense of faith - especially when it seems all is lost - we are enabled to do so by the forces of Uriel.

God's Diversity: The Wisdom of the Angels

Archangel Raphael is depicted as the source of all healing. From the ancient Chaldean[55], Raphael means "God has healed." In *The Book of Enoch*, Raphael "is he who presides over every suffering and every affliction of the sons of men." (Enoch 40:1) The Cayce readings are replete with references that attribute all forms of healing to "the One Force." They affirm that when we use any form of medical treatment, whether it be natural or allopathic[56], we are only placing the body in a receptive state where the healing ability might come *through* to restore harmony to the diseased condition. In this light we can see why the Archangels are not individuals or entities, but powers, forces, and influences which we work with every day. Science and medicine can see that the body has the ability to heal itself, but still it is a mystery how healing happens. Perhaps it is because the Source of all healing, from God through spiritual activity (Raphael), is unseen.

Raphael is also the Archangel who divinely inspires artists. William Blake, a poet and painter of the nineteenth century, had many mystical visions while drawing and engraving works of angels and archangels. Michelangelo, sixteenth-century sculptor, often saw the completed statue locked within the uncut block of marble. He believed he was given the ability to sculpt and paint through divine inspiration.

Very little is written about Archangel Raguel, other than his role which seems to be as a taskmaster for other Archangels as well as commanding the lower angelic realms. In *The Book of Enoch*, Raguel is listed as the guardian Archangel over the "luminaries." According to *The Book of Enoch*, each planet within our solar system - as well as the planets not yet discovered - is a literal heavenly body, an archangel, which radiates inspiration and mystical experience. In this light Raguel is a mentor to these celestial planetary Archangels. Within us, Raguel can be seen as the "guardian" of our seven spiritual centers, our chakras (see chapter 7, "The Angelic Promise - From Adam to Jesus"), regulating and balancing internal conflicts over good and evil.

Archangel Sarakiel is attributed in *The Book of Enoch* with having dominion over the souls who have transgressed against God. He is represented within us as our conscience. When we have erred or sinned, we are made aware of our misdeeds through the forces of Sarakiel, in what Cayce called the throne of our conscience. The readings often said that conscience is the divine inner voice which tells us when we have fallen short or strayed from our spiritual ideals.

Archangel Gabriel (whose name translates to "hero of God"), the most well-known of the Archangels next to Michael, is the messenger who appears in order to reveal God's will - whether it be in the spiritual realms or in the earth. In the New Testament, Gabriel announces to Zacharias that he is to be the father of John the Baptist. Around this same time, Gabriel also announces to Mary that she is to be the mother of Jesus (Luke 1:26-38). Gabriel's role during the time of Christ's appearance on earth was quite extensive. As well as the announcement to Mary and confirmation that her cousin Elizabeth was to be the mother of John the Baptist, Gabriel is also believed to be one of the luminescent angels whom the apostles saw in the tomb after Jesus' crucifixion. In Christian religious thought, Gabriel is the Archangel of resurrection - which explains why he was present in the tomb of Jesus; the power of resurrection is given by the Thrones, through the forces of Gabriel. It makes sense that this angelic being would be present for the first Human who ever overcame death.

Gabriel is also called the "angel of paradise." It is significant here to note that while Jesus was dying upon the cross, He spoke to one of the two thieves He was crucified with, saying, "Today shalt thou be with me in paradise." (Luke 23:43) The Cayce readings defined paradise as a divine state of consciousness which souls gravitate to immediately after death, a place where souls are aware of a great sense of peace, as well as knowing they have just passed from the earth life and yet are aware of being in a contented, expansive state of consciousness. This experience within these realms is similar to the exhilaration that is felt when we are consciously aware that we are dreaming *within a dream* - or what is called "lucid dreaming." In this realm we are surrounded by friends and loved ones.

In art, especially in the paintings of da Vinci, Gabriel is often depicted carrying a lily, Mary's flower, at the annunciation. It is very interesting to note that the coming age or new millennium has been called "the Age of the Lily." When asked to clarify this in a reading, Cayce responded that the lily represents purity, and only the pure in heart would be able to comprehend the full meaning of this great shift in consciousness now upon us. The only thing required of us to fully understand this purity of consciousness is a return to innocence.

When Jesus said that unless we become as children, we will not see the kingdom of God, He was referring to a *state of consciousness*. Bringing this innocent state of being to the forefront of our awareness is a great challenge these days: We are faced with constant news reports of social unrest, crime, earthquakes, and environmental crises, plus a pervasive sense of unease about the days to come. The Cayce readings emphasized to many people that fear is the spiritual opposite of faith. Fear, doubt, and guilt - all of these - seriously undermine our spiritual journey. These negative attitudes and emotions are what must be released and transformed in order for us to perceive the divinity of all life. As was true 2,000 years ago when Gabriel came to announce the birth of Jesus, an age which would be ruled by love and hope, this celestial intelligence has again come to announce through us that we are approaching a new birth of spiritual awakening.

In *The Book of Enoch*, there is a bit of confusion about the role of Ramiel, the seventh leading Archangel in the hierarchy. In one part of the book, Ramiel is the one who presides over mystical vision. In a later section, he is listed among the fallen angels, companions of Lucifer. According to other traditions, Ramiel presides over the coming Judgment Day, when souls will stand before the Thrones and be held accountable for their deeds during their time in earth. Possibly Ramiel is one of the record keepers, part of the angelic forces which rule the akashic records.

In *Return from Tomorrow*, the fascinating account of George Ritchie's nine-minute near-death experience, the author stood before a great Light (which he identified as Christ), which presented every thought, deed, and feeling he had ever experienced during his life on earth. Ritchie said it was not like a movie, but a *living record* of his life, a panoramic and instantaneous playback of his life. Ramiel can be seen as the Archangel who is the guardian of these living life-records. The awareness of this record in our lives today enables us to be cognizant of not only our activities but our thoughts; they are on record just as are deeds. If we become aware that everything we think and do is being made a part of our soul's record, this can awaken a more vital sense of those things in our lives which need transformation.

The lowest order of the third hierarchy comprises the Angels. Even though they are at this level in the celestial hierarchy, their activities and duties are extremely important in the divine interaction between the celestial realms and the earthly realm. Angels bridge the distance between the "seen" and the "unseen," and manifest in a variety of forms. The Cayce readings indicate that Angels are active not only during our earthly lives - providing inspiration, revelation, guidance, and protection - but they also are the messengers who "present" our earthly experiences to higher powers after death, to the "throne of grace and mercy," as the readings put it. For instance, in one reading a businessman, who was taking stock of himself, his relationship to God, as well as his shortcomings, asked:

"In what way have I failed to heed the advice of my Maker, in my actions or deeds, or wherein have I been lacking?"

The sleeping Cayce responded, "Turn within self. No man has the right to find fault with his brother. Neither do the angels that stand before the throne of mercy find fault, but rather *present that which the individual soul has done with his knowledge, his intellect, his*

God's Diversity: The Wisdom of the Angels

understanding. For, thus does the soul find the relationships to the Maker; whether there is the god of light and love and hope, or that which was separated from same that makes for despair, for night, and for those things that do hinder the approach."[57] (Author's italics)

In this instance, the Angels are the "recorders" of our experiences. They present those events to God and we see them after death. Many people who have had near-death experiences report that they find themselves in a place where every thought and deed of their lives is presented to them in a panoramic, instantaneous playback. This life-review often occurs in the presence of Christ, "light-beings," or angels. It is accompanied by a powerful sense of unconditional love, regardless of the individual's misdeeds, faults, and sins. As angels bear the record of our experiences to God, we learn more clearly about our relationship to our Maker. We also learn where we have fallen short and where we have progressed in soul development during life.

The Cayce readings indicate that of all the souls that had been created in the beginning, only *one-third* entered the material world. Many of those who did not enter earthly existence play the roles of guardians, messengers, and bearers of divine decrees for humanity. The many forms of Angels will be discussed at length in chapter 9 ("Our Beloved Guardian Angels").

The divine angelic hierarchy is more than a collection of celestial beings; they are both inner and outer states of consciousness, constantly presenting an opportunity to us for our divine awakening. Now, more than ever, is the awareness dawning within the hearts and minds of people everywhere that the Divine is not a supernatural being somewhere outside to be searched for, but a part of our spiritual ancestry. For many eons, communication from these beings was not comprehensible to our materialistic consciousness. Now, however, the souls of the earth are being roused from a long spiritual sleep and are being readied for the revealing (at the level of the conscious mind) of a great mystery - that we are part and parcel of the great angels of light and love. This is the reality which is unfolding before us like a flower, right now in our world and in our lives.

God's Diversity: The Wisdom of the Angels

Chapter 6

Satan and His Fallen Angels

"It is well to bear in mind that all angels, whatever their state of grace - indeed, no matter how christologically corrupt and defiant - are under God ... " - Gustav Davidson

The Anti-Christ - An Inner Perspective

DURING a philosophy and religion class in the mid-1980s in Virginia Beach, Virginia, J. Everett Irion, one of the foremost authorities on the Edgar Cayce readings' interpretation of the Book of Revelation, was answering questions about the nature of evil. A young woman in his class, who interpreted the Bible literally, wanted specifics about the "anti-Christ."

"Will the anti-Christ rise up from the Mideast and take over the world, commencing the great battle of Armageddon?" she asked pensively. "Or will he be born here in the United States?"

Irion had spent thirty years studying the Book of Revelation before he began teaching a mystical interpretation of the book. This was a frequent question in his classes.

"I will answer your question with a question," Irion responded. "Have you ever experienced a thought, feeling, or attitude you would *not* want to present to God?"

The woman paused and appeared confused. "Well ... of course," she said at last. "I mean - we've all thought bad or mean things or held a grudge here and there. Yes, I've had thoughts I'd be ashamed to present before God."

"The essence of evil, of Satan, of the anti-Christ," Irion answered, "is the sum total of everything that opposes God - in thought, word, deed, experience." He let his words sink in.

"Greed. Hate. Self-condemnation," he continued in a measured pace. "Jealousy. Revenge. Lust. Fear. Guilt. Chaos. Avarice. Confusion. Backbiting. Gossip."

Irion surveyed the class from the podium. "Have you ever felt any of those things?" The class sat in silent reflection. Several heads nodded.

"If the answer is yes," he said, "then *you*, my friends, have entertained the anti-Christ; *you* have helped bring it into being in our world. These are the activities through which the anti-Christ - or Satan - works in the material world."

This idea, which Irion brought into a very personal light that day, was presented in a series of readings Cayce gave in the 1930s on the Book of Revelation. The question was asked, "In what form does the anti-Christ come, spoken of in Revelation?"

"In the spirit of that opposed to the spirit of truth," Cayce answered. "The fruits of the spirit of the Christ are love, joy, obedience, long-suffering, brotherly love, kindness. Against such there is no law. The spirit of hate, the anti-Christ, is contention, strife, fault-finding, love of self, lovers of praise. Those are the anti-Christ, and take possession of groups, masses, and show themselves even in the lives of men."[58]

Irion explained that the angels of darkness have twisted the forces of good into a malevolent spiritual consciousness. The darkness - the anti-Christ - is in direct opposition to that which is good, harmonious, loving. However, the fallen angels operate in the material world through *choices* made by human beings. According to the Cayce readings, when Satan was cast out of heaven by Archangel Michael, he was turned loose in the earth realm and could only do evil through the seduction of the human will. Evil is powerless without the personality's decision to partake of such behavior. Seeking vengeance or harboring hate or causing disruption through jealousy are willful choices that invoke the consciousness of the anti-Christ. It is very easy to look for the darkness outside of ourselves, but not always easy to see it within.

Often the anti-Christ, as referred to in Revelation, is interpreted to be an evil leader who will arise on the world's stage. Many religious sects predict that the anti-Christ will be a person who will wreak havoc as well as destroy governments and eventually the world. Fundamentalist branches of Christianity, which interpret the Bible literally, look for outward signs of the fulfilling of this coming of the anti-Christ. They closely watch government elections and the rise of world leaders. The possibility does exist that out of the collective evil which people purposely manifest in today's world there might be an individual who will come in our time, drawn into the earth through dark desires, injustices, and evil designs of human folly. The evidence of such evil is before us every day on the news: the killings in war-torn Bosnia and Serbia; the religious war between the Catholics and Protestants in Ireland; the slaughter and starvation in Rwanda. The inner city gang wars have devastated South Central Los Angeles and many other cities. These crises reflect the opposite of harmony, love, balance, and trust. These are the worldly manifestations of the anti-Christ. Such evil has also come in the personalities of corrupt world leaders.

Edgar Cayce emphasized the transformative power of attitudes and emotions. We are creating something for our future - individually and collectively - through what we hold and believe in thought. As Cayce asked so many people in the readings, *What are you building?* The responsibility for creating either a harmonious or chaotic future rests solely with us. The readings said that ten people can save a city from destruction by sincerely meditating and praying for peace. Twenty can save a nation.

Satan - The Adversary

Just as we have access to the angels of light, we also have at our disposal a vast, dark reservoir of negative angels. From where do these originate and how do they operate in our world? An eighty-year-old woman received a reading from Cayce and wanted to know the meaning of a vision she had had. In the answer, Cayce details the difference between the workings of the angels of darkness and the angels of light:

"Please explain the visions I have had regarding being shown a vein of gold and an oil deposit near Woodward's Chimney Corner, in Lamb's Spring, Texas."

Edgar Cayce responded, in part, with a question: "Be these rather not those that are as in the influences that arise as emblems in thine own experience, that are as gold precious to the very souls of men, rather than material things?" Cayce counseled the woman that the emblematical meaning was more valuable than gold itself: " ... to thine own life they [are an] emblematical experience. For the angels of light only use material things for emblems, while the angels of death use these as lures that may carry men's souls away. For the Master gave, 'There is a way that seemeth right to the hearts of men, but the end thereof is death and confusion' ... What has given thee thy strength?" Cayce asked. "That ye sought the material things or rather that thou be a handmaid of the Lord?"[59]

Cayce's response does not say that gold and material valuables are evil. He is saying that in this particular woman's case the meaning of the vision was a spiritual call - if she would but heed it - that she had within her a "precious" talent, a faculty, in her soul which would enable her to be a "handmaid" or an example in the material world of spiritual truth and assistance. She also had a tendency to get caught up in material things, and it acted as a distraction which would eventually be destructive to her soul. The choice was strictly up to her.

Cayce identified Satan in the readings in many different forms; for example, Evil One, that Serpent, Devil, the Adversary; its influence was as a collective consciousness, not a personality-self. The Hebrew word for "Satan" translates to "adversary." In the Old Testament's Book of Numbers, "Satan" referred to a job or office rather than an evil being: "And God's anger was kindled because he [Balaam] went: and the angel of the Lord stood in the way for an adversary [Satan] against him." (22:22) In this example, Satan is the angel of the Lord who opposes evil. Divine intercession was needed because Balaam, a prophet of the Midianites, who was eventually slain for his evil, was hired to curse the people of Israel after they took over the land of Moab. Balaam went riding on a donkey to curse the people when suddenly the angel appeared. The angel of the Lord again is in the likeness of Michael: "And the ass [which Balaam sat upon] saw the angel of the Lord standing in the way, and his sword drawn in his hand ... the angel of the Lord stood in a path of the vineyards, a wall being on this side, and a wall on that side." (22:23-24) The angel acted as a "Satan" against Balaam and prevented him from placing the curse upon the people of Israel.

In the New Testament, Peter was called a "Satan" when he tried to dissuade Jesus from going to Jerusalem. "Get thee behind me, Satan," Jesus said. (Luke 4:8) Although Peter thought that he had Jesus' best interests at heart, he was interfering with the fulfilling of Jesus' mission of His death and resurrection. Peter was an adversary of Jesus in this instance. In much of Christian literature and dogma, however, Satan is an evil, fallen archangel who opposes the activities of goodness and light and is the director of all things which oppose God.

Archangel Lucifer - The Light-Bearer

In the beginning, God created Lucifer as an archangel. Lucifer - which means "light-bearer" or light-giver" - has since, however, become synonymous with Satan. According to Gustav Davidson's *Dictionary of Angels*, "The name Lucifer was applied to Satan by St. Jerome and other Church Fathers. Milton in *Paradise Lost* applied the name to the demon of sinful pride. Lucifer is [also] the title and principal character of the epic poem by the Dutch Shakespeare, Vondel (who uses Lucifer in lieu of Satan) ... "[60]

For purposes of chronology, the archangel whom God created

before the fall will be referred to as Lucifer, and after the fall as Satan.

Lucifer was a ruler of the angelic realm of the Cherubim and had dominion over virtually all of the angel kingdoms. He played a very important role in God's creation prior to the great archangelic rebellion and was the tester for the developing souls who were learning to work with their co-creative powers. His role as a "supervisor" among the angels existed long before the earthly realm came into being. In that age all beings were in spirit and consciously aware of being one with God. There was no time, no space; only experience - a great expanding of consciousness into a myriad of creations. Lucifer was charged with ultimate power to oversee and govern God's divine unfoldment.

Dr. M. Scott Peck, in his book *People of the Lie: The Hope for Healing Human Evil,* describes Archangel Lucifer prior to his spiritual rebellion: " ... Satan was God's second-in-command, chief among all His angels, the beautiful and beloved Lucifer. The service it performed in God's behalf was to enhance the spiritual growth of human beings through the use of testing and temptation - just as we test our own children in school so as to enhance their growth. Satan, therefore, was primarily a teacher of mankind, which is why it was called Lucifer, 'the light-bearer.'"[61]

Problems arose when Lucifer fell in love with his own authority and power. The spiritual "fall" from grace was led by this great light-bearer. In the Cayce readings this descent was a journey into selfishness. Lucifer led many of the archangels, angels, and souls deeper into creations which only glorified the individual entities, not God. The Cayce readings don't depict the great descent into selfishness as inherently evil, but that souls merely lost their way - identifying with their creations rather than those of their Creator. Eventually, souls became so invested in their own unique states of consciousness, they forgot from where they had obtained their power. The fallen souls had created their own identities through experimenting with various thought forms and energies. This was the beginning of a sort of self-absorbed "individuality," a state quite normal in our three-dimensional world. But at this period of development in spirit, this individuality represented a complete separation in consciousness from God.

When Archangel Michael and the other governors of the angelic hierarchy who remained in harmony with God tried to intervene, a great battle ensued. At this point in creation, Lucifer had *encouraged* individuality and paved a misguided way which directed souls to become completely individual, minimizing the importance of remaining in tune with or aware of God. Lucifer and the countless souls which followed this plan of selfish individuality rebelled against Michael. That the war is known as the Battle of Light and Darkness is particularly apt, because the harmonious archangels emanated the pure vibrations of light and love of God; while the selfish hordes of Lucifer's followers had become dimmed through their own pursuits, their life-force patterns were dulled and polluted, creating a void or darkness within the realms of light.

John Ronner, in his book *Know Your Angels*, explains the theory of the ancient church teacher Origen, who believed that the varying vibrational patterns of the angels is determined by how close or far from God these angels dwell. "Some intelligences [angels] freely chose to stay close to God, according to plan," he wrote. "They became the highest angels, having ethereal bodies. Others wandered farther away and became lower angels, also with ethereal bodies. Still other beings strayed an even greater distance, becoming physical, fleshly human beings. Those who moved out the farthest became devils, with even coarser, cold bodies."[62]

This passage proposes that evil is only farther distant from God than that which is good. It is not separate from God, but it has removed itself from the Light. According to the Cayce readings, this far-flung reality of evil is "just under" the love of God.

Finally, Lucifer renounced the Light, and his once valuable position of being the adversary to test souls was turned upon God who had brought him into being. Lucifer set up his own kingdom in the farthest reaches of creation, in the biblical "utter darkness" realms of consciousness. This light-bearer now enveloped himself in hate, along with his legions of followers, bent upon opposing everything which represented the oneness with God.

An obvious question is frequently asked: "If God despises and opposes evil, why doesn't He simply do away with Satan and his evil influences?"

The answer is simple. God can't. The Cayce story of the creation of souls reveals that God desired companionship, desired to experience Himself as individualized states of consciousness. To each of these parts of Himself - the souls - He gave free will. Having given souls the ability to choose, the possibility existed that these minute aspects of God - souls, angels, archangels - could defy even God Himself. We don't know for certain if this was part of the original plan: to go out into the world of material things, to immerse oneself in one's own creations, and then of one's own free will to return to God. Lucifer was the first of God's creation to throw a wrench into the harmony of creation. There is great debate as to whether this diversion was an accident or a purposeful experience.

The Cayce readings repeatedly state that it was an error that souls entered such a limiting, three-dimensional state of consciousness, in which their awareness was confined to their own selves and to creations *without* conscious awareness of God. The purpose of the divine plan, according to the readings, is that the souls who forgot their divine heritage have countless opportunities to reawaken from their selfish sleep and return to God through exercising their own free will. This is of such vital importance that the archangels have been put in charge of overseeing this spiritual return. Even though there was a defying of God's original plan for creation, the earth was set up in a way that souls would come to remember their original purpose:

"As has been given," Cayce said, "souls were made to be companions with the Creator. And through error, through rebellion, through contempt, through hatred, through strife, it became necessary then that all pass under the rod; tempted in the fires of flesh; purified, that they may be fit companions for the *glory* that may be thine."[63]

Souls on earth were, as the readings assert, a part of the original rebellion of spirit. But now eons of time later, we are fast approaching a great awakening, the remembrance of God's original plan. On another level, the biblical parable of the Prodigal Son is the story of souls who lost their way (through the rebellion) and then willingly returned "home" to God. In this light, the rebellious fallen angels have operated in a state of amnesia, knowing only their own selfish motives and actions. But even in the lowest state of consciousness the original pattern of God remains. This is beautifully depicted by the Psalmist: "Whither shall I go from thy spirit? or whither shall I flee from thy presence? If I ascend up into heaven, thou art there: if I make my bed in hell, behold, thou art there. If I take the wings of the morning, and dwell in the uttermost parts of the sea; Even there shall thy hand lead me, and thy right hand shall hold me." (Psalm 139:7-10)

If God's presence exists in all creation, even in the realms of hell, as this biblical verse indicates, then it is reasonable to believe that Satan's legions will eventually return to God. The great rebellion or fall of the angels of light might have been part of the great drama of creation for the purpose of experiencing all there is to be experienced in the universe: the light, the darkness, all things in between; and then, full of brilliance, the souls and angels return to God. This viewpoint is difficult to believe when one sees manifestations of evil in society, humanity's inhumanity to itself, the tragedy of hate crimes, war. These are in direct opposition to God's purpose for creation - love, harmony, peace, joy, happiness.

Doorways of Evil

Great responsibility goes along with the process of spiritual and psychic unfoldment. Just as a person would wear protective clothing when going to work in an electrical power plant, we also need to be protected when we delve into the spiritual world. Why? Cayce put it very well in a reading when he said, "As there is, then, a personal savior, there is the personal devil."[64]

Hugh Lynn Cayce conducted investigations into the possible consequences of using Ouija boards and automatic writing. According to his book, *Venture Inward*, people can, unwittingly, become possessed by discarnate evil spirits by use of such devices. He chronicled several frightening cases in which people contacted, through the Ouija board, what appeared to be benevolent beings who dwelt in the higher spiritual realms. After repeated communications, however, these beings took over the people conducting psychic experiments and turned their existence into a living nightmare. Whether these invading influences were part of the collective unconscious mind or separate evil entities is irrelevant. The end result was disastrous: The individual's free will had been given over to some unseen power which intended great harm.

"The danger with Ouija boards," Hugh Lynn said in a private conversation with the author, "is that they are so *easy* to use. It takes very little effort to open that 'doorway' into what Dad [Edgar Cayce] called the 'borderland.' This area is where earthbound souls are gathered, looking for an entrance into the earth by either automatic writing, Ouija boards, or mediumship."

However, there are some people who have had great spiritual success with using Ouija boards. Author-medium Jane Roberts wrote many fascinating books based on her psychic relationship with a discarnate entity named Seth, who spoke through her and dictated books. Her initial contact with him was through an Ouija board. It is the *indiscriminate* approach to them and to mediumship, which can result in rare instances, that Hugh Lynn documented in *Venture Inward*.

Improper meditation can also lead to psychic openings and to undesirable psychic influences and attacks. A number of people came to Cayce with disturbing experiences with discarnate entities. The readings indicated that this resulted from an improper or premature opening of the body's spiritual centers by practicing a form of meditation which created an avenue through which these spirits could influence and cause problems of possession.

One woman who was experiencing psychotic episodes with delusions of persecution wrote to Cayce. The subsequent reading indicated that she had opened herself to possession through "study" (probably a form of meditation): "It is indicated that the body is a supersensitive individual entity who has allowed itself through study, through opening the centers of the body, to become possessed ... "[65] (There is a safe method of meditation recommended by the Cayce readings discussed in chapter 9, "Our Beloved Guardian Angels.")

Although the possession cases in *Venture Inward* didn't result in an exorcism, the clergy was called in and prayers were invoked to free them from the evil influences. "The frightening thing about these cases," Hugh Lynn wrote, "is that they can be duplicated by the thousands from the case histories of present-day inmates of mental institutions all over the world."[66] Hugh Lynn Cayce believed that many inmates, diagnosed as hopelessly insane in U.S. mental hospitals, had unwittingly opened themselves to psychic interference through the use of automatic writing and Ouija boards.

"The voices they are hearing," Hugh Lynn said, "are not part of a psychotic delusion; they're real. These people opened the door of their unconscious minds and can't close it. They need spiritual help, not just psychological and medical attention. A great number of them are indeed possessed by discarnate entities."

There are over forty references in the Cayce readings to actual possession by discarnate spirits. In some instances, this resulted from an individual dabbling in psychic experiments without proper knowledge or preparation. One woman was receiving what she felt to be angelic or cosmic messages from the spiritual realms. She sought Edgar Cayce for spiritual advice in his readings:

"To further my work in possible radio reception of cosmic messages, should I attempt to train myself in automatic handwriting, or use a medium?"

Cayce responded in the negative on both counts: "As has been indicated, rather than automatic writing or a medium, turn to the voice within! If this then finds expression in that which may be given to the self in hand, by writing, it is well; but not that the hand be guided by an influence outside of itself. For the universe, God, is within. Thou art His. Thy communion with the cosmic forces of nature, thy communion with thy Creator, is thy birthright! Be satisfied with nothing less than walking with Him!"[67]

In this instance, Cayce cautions against communing with the higher or discarnate spirits and entities. He advises to seek "the voice within," that limitless consciousness which is in direct communion with God. The problem with automatic writing, according to the Cayce readings, is that the person who uses it as a psychic tool will never develop beyond the source of the information or higher than the entity directing. Yet, if the information is from the *inspirational* dimensions within, Cayce said that this develops the soul; this is from the inmost part of the soul which is connected to God.

Fallen Angels and Free Will

Many religious doctrines hold that the fallen angels who went astray are not necessarily earthly people, but have great influence in the lives of earthly souls. In this light, Satan and his followers are a perfect creation gone perfectly bad, inherently evil and never to be redeemed, nor can they return to God. Their sole purpose is to defy God and distract earthly souls from remembering their divine origins. Author Malachi Martin in *Hostage to the Devil* views the "fall" of Satan and his legions of angels as an inexorable, unforgivable movement of consciousness which God Himself cannot rectify. He sees the fallen angels as being beyond hope, their wills hopelessly twisted and condemned by their own selves. All that was love within them is turned to hate and cannot be redeemed. Whereas God represents life, light, hope, joy, and harmony, the fallen angels are hellbent on destruction, chaos, hopelessness, fear, and guilt. These are the powers through which the forces of darkness, Satan, operate in the material world.

In his exploration of evil, demonic possession, and exorcism, Martin conveys the definite impression that just as there are powerful angels of good and light which help bring into our world the awareness of God's love, majesty, and beauty, there also exist the corresponding opposite demons which manifest hate, selfishness, prejudice, and mayhem. The reality of malevolent angels is difficult to dispute after reading his exhaustive book on the subject of the demonic. Although there are many forms of evil entities, demons, and fallen angels, Martin asserts that they are all attributes of one evil source - Satan.

The Cayce readings indicate a philosophy that souls always have free will to choose to do evil or good. God's creatures were not intended to be automated robots who would blindly follow His commands, but it is God's desire that they be willful beings who *choose* to be one with Him. In many instances the readings emphasized that God has not willed that any soul should perish nor be lost, but has with every temptation prepared a way of escape. With our free will, we can always succumb to such temptations and fall under the umbrella of evil influences. On the other hand, we always have at our disposal the help of the great angels and archangels - a divine promise, as stated in the Bible.

"For he shall give his angels charge over thee, to keep thee in all thy ways. They shall bear thee up in their hands, lest thou dash thy foot against a stone." (Psalm 91:11-12) The determining factor is how much we *believe* in this promise. If we reach a point of despair where we are no longer listening to the voice of intuition - a point, for example, where we have given up due to material circumstances - then we have cut ourselves off from the help and hope which emanates from the angelic kingdom.

One of the most reassuring ideas offered to us in the Bible and repeated often in the Cayce readings is that we are *always* in the presence of God, no matter how distracted we become by the cares of the world. But we must, of our own free will, call upon God and His angels to help us. God cannot intervene where He is not wanted nor invited. The injustice which humankind will do to its brothers and sisters, for instance, has nothing whatsoever to do with what God wills for us. God gave us the ultimate gift: His own ability to create whatever He desired. This truly is a double-edged sword - especially when we choose to be diabolical to one another. We create our own adversity through operating under the law of karma: what we put out comes back to us, sometimes a hundredfold.

There is the misguided notion that God doles out karma, watching and waiting for the opportunity to smite wayward souls. But rather humanity's adversity becomes God's opportunity. People pass through trials and tribulations specifically so that they might rely on the God unseen. Yet, He cannot stop what has been willed by humanity. When God gave the soul free will, He gave it a very powerful tool: we may use our will *by choice* to live a life in harmony with God, or we may use that powerful faculty to wreak havoc and destruction.

The Cayce readings indicate that God is *lonely* for the souls who chose individual experience without respect to His consciousness. There is a waiting, a watching, and, when necessary, intervention in our lives from His angels who come to remind us of whom we belong. The issue at hand is whether or not we are listening to these signs; our faithful God is calling us, in love, to return to the domain of consciousness with Him.

God and World Atrocities

How often have we heard the question concerning the Holocaust: *Why would God allow such a thing to happen?* God has nothing to do with such atrocities. Because we were given free will, even God Himself cannot halt what we choose to do to one another. In a time in which humanity vowed never to allow another Holocaust to happen, we see the evidence of "ethnic cleansing" in Rwanda, Bosnia, and Serbia; races, tribes, and nationalities systematically tortured and killed. In these instances can we see what Cayce meant when he said that the anti-Christ can take possession of individuals, groups, organizations - even races. It appears obvious that the leaders who advocate hate, prejudice, and genocide are of the league of the fallen angels.

A powerful soul named Adolf Hitler seemed to have the entirety of the blessings of Satan himself at his disposal to attempt to carry out his malignant vision called "the final solution" of exterminating the Jews during World War II. The power to command hundreds of thousands of Nazis to commit murder was indeed a malevolent power from the realms of hell itself. Yet, there are stories from this tragedy which indicate that there is a divine light even in the darkest night. As a medical doctor working at the end of World War II to liberate the concentration camps, George Ritchie, author of *Return to Tomorrow*, found love amid the hatred. He found something which even the most malevolent of fallen angels could not touch.

Dr. Ritchie assisted the inmates of a concentration camp near Wuppertal, Poland, in receiving medical attention when Germany surrendered to the Allies in 1945. One such inmate helped Ritchie treat the starving prisoners from the camp. "Wild Bill," as Ritchie called him, appeared to have recently arrived at the camp prior to Germany's surrender. He seemed healthy, bright, optimistic, and in good spirits. Wild Bill always had time to help at least one more inmate at the long day's end. His energy seemed boundless. He became a valuable resource for Ritchie and the rest of the medical team in helping the former prisoners find their families, in offering translations and doing paperwork. Dr. Ritchie was astounded when he learned that Wild Bill had been a concentration camp inmate since 1939! Ritchie wrote the following in his book, *Return from Tomorrow*:

> "For six years he [Wild Bill] had lived on the same starvation diet, slept in the same airless and disease-ridden barracks as everyone else, but without the least physical or mental deterioration. Perhaps even more amazing, every group in the camp looked on him as a friend ... Only after I'd been at Wuppertal a number of weeks did I realize what a rarity this was in a compound where different nationalities of prisoners hated each other almost as much as they did the Germans."[68]

Ritchie believed that the secret to Wild Bill's survival was love. In the face of great persecution and hatred from the Germans, Wild Bill learned love and forgiveness. According to Ritchie, Wild Bill had lived in the Jewish section of Warsaw with his wife, two daughters, and three little boys.

> " 'When the Germans reached our street,' he said, 'they lined everyone against a wall and opened up with machine guns. I begged to be allowed to die with my family, but because I spoke German they put me in a work camp ... I had to decide right then ... whether to let myself hate the soldiers who had done this. It was an easy decision, really. I was a lawyer. In my practice I had seen too often what hate could do to people's

minds and bodies. Hate had just killed the six people who mattered most to me in the world. I decided then that I would spend the rest of my life - whether it was a few days or many years - loving every person I came in contact with.' Loving every person ... this was the power that had kept a man well in the face of every privation."[69]

Wild Bill made a *choice* to not hate those who had persecuted him. He realized that the very evil which killed his family thrived on hate. For Wild Bill to react in kind with the Germans would have created a pact of evil and continued the chain of hate. In his ability to love, Bill ascended from the darkness to the light and was freed. In doing so, he not only survived the Holocaust, but he miraculously retained his health. How? His choosing to love opened a channel or way through which the Divine could help him. In hatred, there is no channel of light, no divine intervention, no help available. There is only access to more evil influences which perpetuate and flourish in such emotions. Love breaks the chain of whatever power the angels of darkness have. Edgar Cayce once said in a reading that it was easy to love one's friends; the real challenge is loving the enemy; the people who hurt, betray, or deceive us. The readings went so far as to say that until we can see the Christ in the most vile person, we have not yet begun to grow spiritually. This indeed is a challenge for all of us.

The Battle of Good and Evil

Some wise but unknown source once said that a thousand souls of darkness do not have the power of one soul of light. Looking at the life and death of Jesus of Nazareth, we can see that it was a mass effort of evil which carried out His crucifixion. Yet, that evil could not hold Him in the shackles of death because Jesus *loved those who hated Him*. Facing those who betrayed Him, Jesus even asked God to forgive them; to forgive them because if they'd really known what they were doing, they would not have done it. He forgave them as one would forgive unruly children. In this light, evil is ignorance and unknowing; it is - as Cayce put it - goodness misapplied. The redemption of evil may only be a matter of awakening to spiritual truth.

In our present time, we do not have to look very far to see the effects of evil in our society. If there is a *modus operandi* of Satan and his fallen angels, it is the spirit of hate. Truly the most devastating of the attitudes and emotions to be experienced in our lives, hate destroys, condemns, avenges itself, promotes ignorance, and feeds upon fear. It has become so prominent in our present-day society that a new and dark phrase has been coined by our news agencies: "hate crimes." Hate flourishes where there is ignorance, prejudice, and fear. As Cayce said, these dark angelic activities of Satan can possess individuals and groups, divide the races, religions, and sexes.

The readings assert that the activity of Satan was one of the main reasons Christ came in body into the earth:

"Thus do we see and comprehend why it was necessary that He, the Son, the Maker, the Creator, come unto His own; who in their blindness, selfishness, hates, spites, have brought and do bring about those influences that keep the heart of man from seeking the way."[70]

Christ incarnated so that there would be manifest in our world a presence, a power, a love which would overcome any acts or manifestations of evil. Cayce's view of the destiny of Satan and his fallen angels was that through light and understanding all would eventually find their way back to their Creator. This concept differs vastly from the idea that evil is unchangeable and unredeemable.

There was a time, however, according to biblical lore, when Satan was not an essential evil adversary of God, but an ally. In the Book of Job, God is engaged in dialogue with Satan, who came before Him with the "sons of God" (the first order of created souls who remained in harmony with God - see chapter 7), and Satan reports that he has been treading "to and fro in the earth." In the biblical account, God attests to the purity of Job and wagers a bet that he would never

Satan and His Fallen Angels

renounce Him. In a bizarre sort of chess game, God agrees that Satan can perform any test of faith he chooses, but he is not to hurt Job himself. It is interesting to note that when God and Satan were reasoning out their game plan for Job, God said to Satan, "Behold, all that he [Job] hath is in thy power ... " (1:12) Satan then goes on a rampage, killing the servants, destroying Job's home, and stealing his cattle. But Job would not renounce God.

The Book of Job indicates that the angels and archangels ("sons of God") spent time in creative activity and then would return to report their deeds to God. For example, after Job's first test by Satan, the Bible says, "Again there was a day when the sons of God came to present themselves before the Lord, and Satan came also among them to present himself before the Lord." (2:1) It is reasonable to deduce that Satan was still within God's grace during this period. " ... to present himself before the Lord" doesn't indicate that Satan was banished to utter darkness or that he hated God. Satan was acting as Job's "adversary" or coach under God's direction.

The God of the Book of Job even seems to be baiting Satan at one point to further challenge His servant: "Hast thou considered my servant Job, that there is none like him in the earth, a perfect and an upright man, one that feareth God, and escheweth evil? and still he holdeth fast his integrity, although thou movedst me against him, to destroy him without cause." (2:3) Satan seems to lightly shrug this off and announces that when a man's life is in danger, he will always renounce God under duress.

God again resumes this chess match: "And the Lord said unto Satan, Behold, he is in thine hand; but save his life." (2:6) So Satan does what he does best: wreaked havoc in Job's life, made him sick with boils, until Job cursed the day he was born. He lost his family, his health, and all that was dear to him in life, but he did not speak ill of God, nor did he renounce Him. In the latter portion of the Book of Job, God bestows upon him twice as much as he had ever lost.

The Cayce readings indicate that all souls will be tested so that they may be worthy to eventually be co-creators with God again. Part of this testing is the choice of renouncing all that abhors love, peace, harmony. How can we choose love, peace, and harmony if we are not also faced with its exact opposite in our lives? Every day is an opportunity to choose what we will serve - the source of good or of evil.

It is further interesting to note that Edgar Cayce called the years of 1958 to 1998 the times of testing and crisis. All souls during this time will be presented with circumstances which would test faith, patience, endurance, forgiveness, love. This time period is particularly relevant because it represents a sort of cosmic "final exam," after which the so-called new age of Aquarius will have begun.

There has never been a time in the earth's history, according to the Cayce readings, as our present for soul development opportunities. Part of this challenge has to do with battling our own inner forces of good and evil, choosing which to follow. As we've seen, the experiences of people with angels are increasing, signifying the potential of a great ascent in human consciousness. Is it any wonder that there are more souls on earth today than ever before in history? The Cayce readings say that the opportunities for growth and soul development during this forty-year period will not be seen again for thousands of years.

The importance of these days lies in examining the *spirit* in which we do what we do in our lives. If we don't awaken to the expansive spiritual opportunities at our door, then we may descend into the depths of confusion, fear, regret, hopelessness. Although we may not realize it, by abandoning hope we actually embrace the darkness and its companion angels. Just as there are angels of light, love, peace, and harmony, there are also the devils of strife, contention, fear, and regret. We draw these influences around us, not just by our deeds, but also by our thoughts and feelings.

The Seduction of Deceit - Evil in Everyday Life

Cambridge theologian C.S. Lewis wrote that we are more at risk from *devils* than the Devil. Lewis saw the fallen state of the dark angels, not in the realm of hell, fire, and brimstone, but in the well-lit offices of political figures gone bad: "The greatest evil ... is not done even in concentration camps and labour camps ... But it is conceived and ordered ... in clean, carpeted, warmed, and well-lighted offices, by quiet men with white collars and cut fingernails and smooth-shaven cheeks who do not need to raise their voice ... my symbol for Hell is something like the bureaucracy of a police state or the offices of a thoroughly nasty business concern ... Bad angels, like bad men, are entirely practical."[71]

In this light we can see why much of the evil influences remain unseen with no outward appearance of a devil. The activities of Satan and his maligned followers are deceitful in that they work *through* individuals, groups, organizations. In earlier times, Satan has been rendered in art as a beautiful seducer with the face of a cherub. When one sees these beautiful paintings, by Raphael for example, there is a momentary sense of unreality. We expect the Evil One to appear with the images of our worst nightmare. If the people who do evil had a countenance of a forked tongue, plus horns and a tail, how much influence could they wield in the affairs of humanity? Not much. We would recognize the fallen angels immediately. Instead, we become aware of the nature of evil by deeds, motives, activities. As Jesus said, " ... by their fruits ye shall know them." (Matthew 7:20) Still, those who commit the most evil of acts have within them the potential for good. The original pattern of divinity which was granted by God in the beginning does not change, but it can be covered over with the depraved nature of evil.

Hugh Lynn Cayce asked his father how all things can come from one divine Source and yet be clearly manifestations of evil in our world. "In relation to the oneness of all force," Hugh Lynn asked, "explain the popular concept of the Devil, seemingly substantiated in the Bible by many passages of Scripture."

The sleeping Cayce responded, "In the beginning, celestial beings. We have first the Son [Christ], then the other sons or celestial beings [angels] that are given their force and power. Hence that force which rebelled in the unseen forces (or in spirit), that came into activity, was that influence which has been called Satan, the Devil, the Serpent; they are one. That of *rebellion!* Hence, when man in any activity rebels against the influences of good he harkens to the influence of evil rather than the influence of good ... Evil is rebellion. Good is the Son of life, of light, of truth; and the Son of light, of life, of truth, came into physical being to demonstrate and show and lead the way for man's ascent to the power of good over evil in a material world."[72]

This reading indicates that whenever people go against that which is good or seek to deceive, then they are making a channel through which the forces of Satan can operate in a material world. The original battle of the angels of light with the angels of darkness is now fought upon the battleground of the human psyche. All that happened in spiritual realms of consciousness have their pattern imprinted upon our souls. As we are miniature replicas of the entirety of the spiritual universe, we also contain the activities which went on in the unseen realms. The battle between Michael and Lucifer is now the battle within of selflessness versus selfishness. This war spans the eons of time that souls have occupied the earth.

The Fall of the Angels - A Brief History

The ancient *Book of Enoch*, once a part of our Bible, details at great length the ruling angels which are capable of good and evil in the affairs of humanity. What is sobering about this *Book of Enoch* is that these were not celestial beings at all. They came to earth in physical bodies, procreated, created war and dissension. This concept was very difficult for the early church leaders to accept, that some of the angels actually could be living in the world. The book was eventually denounced and banned, and excluded from what we now know as the Bible. However, in 1773, a text of *The Book of Enoch* was found by James Bruce, a Scottish explorer, in Ethiopia. The book was subsequently taken to Great Britain where Dr. Richard Laurence, a professor of Hebrew, translated the first English-speaking version of it.

The Book of Enoch chronicles the first of the fallen angels' descent into the earth. The Cayce readings on the creation of the world parallel Enoch's vision. After the earth became generally populated, the angels became enticed by the physical beauty of women and became enmeshed in the material world through lust. Several sources agree with this theory. John Ronner, author of *Know Your Angels*, explained the Enochian viewpoint about the fall of angels:

" ... some of heaven's choir members eyed lovely mortal women, were overcome with lust, and defiled their holiness by having intercourse. This forbidden sex sired a race of terrible half-breed giants that plagued the earth. For their misdeeds, the angels fell and received terrible divine punishment."[73]

The Book of Genesis depicted the fall in similar fashion: "And it came to pass, when men began to multiply on the face of the earth, and daughters were born unto them, That the sons of God saw the daughters of men that they were fair; and they took them wives of all which they chose ... There were giants in the earth in those days; and also after that, when the sons of God came in unto the daughters of men, and they bare children to them, the same became mighty men ... " (Genesis 6:1-2, 4)

There is nothing in the literature which refers to these "giants" as human beings, but they were creatures and beasts with human-like features. The Cayce readings indicate at this point that souls were entering into the earth in a variety of forms: centaurs, Cyclops, mermaids, and a host of other freakish creations. The figures in Greek mythology were not fiction at all, according to the readings; instead, mythology chronicles the actual history of the early attempts of souls to push themselves into the material world in imperfect bodies. The purpose was simple: individuality and self-expression. The problem was that the earth had its own evolutionary laws; it, too, was evolving toward perfection in the plant, mineral, and animal kingdoms in a very different form than the spiritual evolution God had intended for souls. However, once the souls became attracted to the material world and began to mingle with its elements, they became subject to the laws governing the earth and its evolution.

The once great unlimited powers of the angels in the celestial realms became limited within the confines of material life when the souls chose to take on form and become a part of the world. The sensual world was the attracting force which drew the souls into the earth.

According to *The Book of Enoch*, an angel whose description is very similar to that of Satan, Azazyel, led 200 of the angels to cohabitate with the mortals already arrived in earth and working out their spiritual mission. The angels, under Azazyel's direction, taught the mortals to fashion swords, knives, and weapons of war; instructed the women in creating and wearing cosmetics; and showed them how to make jewelry from precious stones. Azazyel's group instructed humans in knowledge which had never been attained in earth prior to the appearance of these dark angels: Amazarak who taught how to use sorcery and Barkayal who taught astrology.

While today there is widespread use of the above activities, in the ancient days these developments had come too early; humankind was not yet ready for the power which would be wielded from such knowledge. These technologies acted as distractions for the developing souls. It might have been like giving small children destructive weapons to play with. The souls got distracted from their lessons with their "toys" and went on a rampage, trying out the new and mysterious activities taught to them. In any case, the end result of the angels' teachings was disastrous: "Impiety increased; fornication multiplied; and they transgressed and corrupted all their ways ... And men, being destroyed, cried out; and their voice reached heaven." (Enoch 8:2, 9)

At this point, the calamity going on within the earth's realm drew the attention of the archangels Michael, Uriel, and Gabriel. They eventually intervened and forcibly removed the rebellious fallen angels from the earth's influence and imprisoned them in the celestial. Enoch goes into great detail in his revelatory vision. To cleanse the earth of the evil doings of the fallen angels, God sent the great Flood, which is detailed in Genesis.

The length of time from the advent of the fallen angels to the eventual removal of their influence spanned eons - 200,000 years in fact. During this period the Cayce readings gave great detail to the conflict of the "sons of Belial" (the fallen angels) with the "Children of the Law of One" (souls of humanity who came to earth to regain their original divine heritage). There are several references in the Bible which indicate that Belial, if not another name for Satan, is an angel in close proximity with the chief of the angels of darkness. In the Book of Deuteronomy, "the children of Belial" go off to seek other gods instead of God. (13:13) In the Book of Judges the "sons of Belial" abuse and rape a woman. (19:22) In II Samuel, a man accuses and curses King David of being a "man of Belial." (16:7) St. Paul makes reference to Belial in II Corinthians: " ... and what communion hath light with darkness? And what concord hath Christ with Belial? or what part hath he that believeth with an infidel?" (6:14-15)

The activities of the children of Belial were in opposition to the spiritual ideals of the Children of the Law of One. " ... the disturbing forces grew to be factors to be reckoned with," Cayce said, "between the Children of the Law of One and the sons of Belial. For, these were the representation of what in the present experiences would be termed good and evil, or a spiritual thought and purpose and a material thought or desire or purpose."[74]

The Influence of the Fallen Angels Today

Since the beginning of humanity's advent into the earth, there has always been those of "Belial" and those of the "Light." The determining differences between God's angelic hierarchy and Satan's fallen angels is their intent, purpose, and desire. The importance is not so much what these beings *are* - it is rather a matter of what they *do*. John Ronner writes in *Know Your Angels*: " ... Origen of Alexandria, probably the leading biblical scholar of the ancient Christian church, believed that whether a being is an angel, human or devil depends on how far it decided to drift away from God's presence."[75]

There is a tendency to believe in the fallen angels or demons only when one hears of hauntings or in cases of exorcism. These manifestations are indeed rare and do not account for a large percentage of evil influences in the earth. Evil manifests in a variety of ways, just as virtue appears in countless forms. The important point is that evil or disharmony is a *choice;* the fallen are only in that state of existence when the choice is made to twist creative abilities into destructive ones. Where there is manipulation, oppression, war, famine, governmental control of religious belief, there exist the fallen ones.

A promise, however, in Cayce's readings indicates that the ultimate destruction to be wrought upon those who willingly do evil will be upon themselves. This is a law which a merciful God put in place to protect the majority who wish to do good and evolve toward their status as co-creators with God. In our perception of time, however, it may appear that an evil empire or government flourishes for many years before its end. In God's mind, however, it is merely but the passage of a day before they are brought under subjection by His angels of light.

Satan and His Fallen Angels

Chapter 7

The Angelic Promise - From Adam to Jesus

"And so it is written, The first man Adam was made a living soul; the last Adam was made a quickening spirit ... The first man is of the earth, earthy: the second man is the Lord from heaven." -
I Corinthians 15:45, 47

The Story of Amilius

THE Angelic From a metaphysical viewpoint, the entire Bible is an extended allegorical story of our long spiritual journey "home." Edgar Cayce was a great student of the Bible; he read it through once for every year of his life - sixty-seven times. When he wasn't giving psychic readings, Cayce loved to teach Sunday school, and his classes at the Presbyterian church were often "standing room only" - with children as well as adults in attendance. The waking psychic abilities Cayce possessed enabled him to glimpse the hidden truths of the Bible and shed light upon its spiritual meaning. His family and close associates also asked a number of fascinating questions about the days of Genesis and the creation of humanity, which were answered in their readings.

Then Cayce subsequently gave more specific readings on the early days of creation that span the entire epoch in detail from Adam through the life of Jesus. These readings have helped countless investigators, researchers, and theologians in their understanding of the Bible and indicate that the preparation period for the coming of Jesus into the earth was actually *millions* of years.

During the great chaos of the early epoch of the creation of souls - the age of "giants in the earth," according to the Book of Genesis (6:4)

- the earth was filled with all imaginable forms of inhabitants. During this pre-Genesis period, Satan and his legions had taken leave of the lighter realms of angels and made their abode in the unfinished earth and in other areas. A promise, however, was born in the kingdoms of the angels that all those souls who had forgotten God and had become lost would eventually be led back by way of a divinely ingenious plan.

The Book of Genesis begins at this point, establishing it as the beginning of time: "And the earth was without form, and void; and darkness was upon the face of the deep." (1:2)

The darkness represents the separation of souls from their awareness of their Creator - a darkness of consciousness. Satan and his legions were the embodiment of that darkness. Although eons had already passed since the souls had taken on identities fashioned by their own creations, this point in Genesis is the beginning of a divine plan, the start of a long process through time and space in which the sleeping souls would be awakened. Thomas Sugrue, in the "Philosophy" chapter of *There Is a River*, detailed the dilemma of the souls at that time:

"The earth was an expression of divine mind with its own laws, its own plan, its own evolution. Souls, longing to feel the beauty of the seas, the winds, the forest, the flowers, mixed with them and expressed themselves through them. They also mingled with the animals and made, in imitation of them, thought forms: they played at creating; they imitated God. But it was a playing, an imitating, that interfered with what had already been set in motion, and thus the stream of mind carrying out the plan for earth gradually drew souls into its current. They had to go along with it, in the bodies they had themselves created.

"They were strange bodies: mixtures of animals, a patch-work of ideas about what it would be pleasant to enjoy in flesh. Down through the ages fables of centaurs, Cyclops, etc., have persisted as a relic of this beginning of the soul's tenancy of earth."[76]

The Angelic Promise - From Adam to Jesus

The plight of those who had become trapped in their own darkness were seen and heard by one particular, very special soul. Called Amilius in the Cayce readings, this soul had traveled through many universal experiences, but had never left the Light nor gotten entangled in the ways of Satan. According to the readings, this was the first soul who had ventured forth and *returned* to the conscious presence of God.

Upon seeing the calamity of earthly souls, Amilius promised God he would journey with them to fully understand their individualized state of consciousness in the material world and help them remember their divine origins. Amilius promised he would lead the way to set souls free from the material distractions which the powers and angels of darkness imposed. He would gradually descend into the depths of material life and then be a leader on the long road back to the harmony, to the heaven of God consciousness. This path was the only way he knew to bring back fellow souls to remembrance of their divine heritage. He could only do this by becoming one of the forgetful souls himself. A noble and loving mission indeed.

It was a great plan, and Amilius had the blessings and promise of the celestial guardians, the archangels, the Creator Himself, that he would not make this journey alone. The sons and daughters of God - 144,000 of them - would also assist Amilius in becoming mortal. They would journey with him to the earthly realms and join in the great mission to rouse the sleeping souls who were alive with desire, but asleep in spirit. It was a task which would not be easy for him and those beings who would put on mortality; for they would be subject to the earthly laws of evolution and some lessons would have to be learned so slowly. If the great sons and daughters of God who would put on flesh bodies became enamored with the sensuality of the material world, they, too, might become hypnotized with those things of the world, requiring millennia to repair. Even so, this consideration had its place in the plan of redemption - for if the souls did forget, they would have the intimate guidance of the higher angels and archangels who never left the presence of God, who would, at every turn in the material world, remind them of their original mission.

Until the mission was complete, until every soul who had forgotten God returned, the angels from on high would stand in eternal vigilance, guarding and directing not only the individual souls, but groups, nations, and races. Each angel would have its own particular job in assisting the souls who still remembered God as well as those who had forgotten. The angels' role would be as messengers of the incarnate souls, and the means for divining messages would include apparitions, dreams and visions, omens and signs.

The Creation of Humankind

In order for Amilius to enter into the earth, he would need to create for himself a new kind of body which would not be like the monstrous creations the fallen ones had made for themselves. This vehicle, which would carry his soul in the earth, would originate from the very mind of God; a body which would be made of every element of the earth kingdom and yet have the spiritual circuitry to enable it to remain in contact with the realms of God and the angels. In this way, this new being would be of materiality and yet also of God. It would contain earth and spirit - a harmony never before realized. This would be an artwork most divine, created from the highest realms of God; for He longed for the souls who had gone astray to return home. Through this means, souls could develop and grow spiritually in the earth and bring in limitless talents and creativity which originated in the spirit realms among the angels.

God worked through Amilius to gradually create, in the realms of spirit, a design for this new body. As the pattern for the body was nearing completion, there were created seven spiritual centers or circuits. These centers would enable the soul to attune itself to the highest realms of the celestial hierarchy and from there to receive creativity, talents, inspiration, and divine guidance while living in the earth. (See Figure 2.)

THE SEVEN SPIRITUAL CENTERS

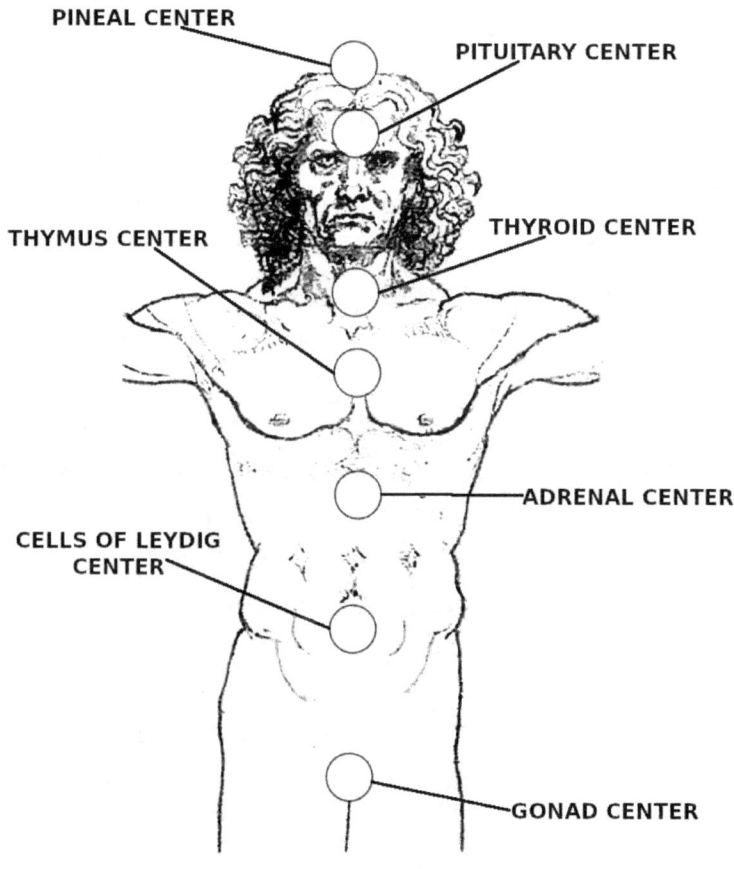

Figure 2

These centers, called *chakras* in Sanskrit, created a perfect union between the material and spirit worlds. All elements of the earthly and heavenly kingdoms were contained within the body which would house the soul. The four lower chakras corresponded to the four elements of fire, water, earth, and air. The three higher centers corresponded to the highest realms of God: Creator Spirit, Son Spirit, and Holy Spirit. Their very pattern, imprinted within the spiritual consciousness of the soul-body, insured a potential that the soul would never be out of attunement with the Divine, as long as it didn't choose to cut itself off from higher knowledge. This situation, however, would still be a possibility because the soul would retain and manifest its free will in the earth.

Chaos had resulted when souls became trapped in the imperfect bodies of monstrosities because their sensuous desires had cut them off from communion with God. In this new body, however, a soul could always be one step from remembering its divine purpose through those indwelling spiritual centers.

As God existed in a triune[77] of consciousness, so the new human in the earth would also exist with a body, a mind, a spirit. Each element could have separate functions, but would be contained within the one body. The triune replica would be this: First, the *soul* would be the source of all spiritual knowledge and activity in the earth. Second, the *mind* would draw from the soul to create circumstances through the power of thought. This was a very sophisticated feature, for the mind could bring into the material world anything it chose to concentrate upon. Yet upon the mind was set the *perfect* awareness of God - what the readings called the *Christ Consciousness* - although it would have to be continually awakened by the will through meditation and prayer. The soul could then draw from the Divine itself and bring it into activity in earth. Third would be the *physical body* itself, the new vehicle with which to carry out the mission of the soul and mind.

This new race of beings would bring the powers of heaven into the earth. The animal kingdom had already been in existence for a long time prior to the arrival of humans, yet the animals did not possess the power to choose. They were lower than the new race about to be born, for the souls of humankind would bring with them the powers of free will and choice. The new physical race would always draw its mental and spiritual sustenance from the unseen realms of the angels.

The Angelic Promise - From Adam to Jesus

At last, Amilius had completed the soul pattern of the body, which would be a channel for entities to redeem the material world. It was a glorious moment of the beginning, the beginning of the journey to divine remembrance. The Bible depicts this event as the true origin of the world, "When the morning stars sang together, and all the sons of God shouted for joy." (Job 38:7) The morning stars were the angels who rejoiced that a way had been prepared so that the rest of the celestial family would return to the fold of God. The vigilant participation of the angels would always exist as promised. They would always be there to wait, inspire, awaken, direct, at every turn of humanity's development.

The entity, known as Amilius in the spiritual realms, would be called Adam, and his coming was glorious in the earth, for in him hope was born as a physical being, a leader, a way-shower. As promised, he did not travel to the earth alone. The Cayce readings confirm that 144,000 souls followed the pattern of Adam, created the humanoid bodies we now occupy, and the races were born. These were *new races;* they did not have the monstrous appendages of the so-called mythological creatures. This race would reproduce only after its own kind. Although it might take hundreds of thousands of years for the monstrosities created by the fallen souls to become extinct, the fallen ones would eventually all incarnate to earth into the pattern of Adam's body, built by God for Amilius.

In building Adam's body in the earth, it was necessary that there be a feminine counterpart. This was done, according to the readings, by Adam going into meditation and traveling in an out-of-body state to the realms where spiritual creation was taking place - the realms of the angels. There, under the direction of God, the soul of Adam separated itself into two. In the story of Genesis, Eve being created from the "rib of Adam" actually refers to the feminine side of his soul manifesting as an individual. In Hebrew "rib" translates as "side."

Edgar Cayce elaborated about this unique manifestation of the male and female counterparts in a lecture to his Bible class: " ... God created man and woman first as one, in *spirit*. Then male and female in flesh. As the mind became aware of its duality in matter, there was the necessity for the positive and negative force to be separate, yet cooperative."[78]

The other souls did likewise, and male and female bodies were created upon the earth. That magnificent creation saw the advent on five major continents of the five races: black, white, yellow, red, brown. Each soul would experience - through many eons in the earth - the development of each race. At the time of Adam and Eve's advent into the Garden of Eden, hundreds of thousands of sons and daughters of God were also manifesting in the earth at the same time.

The Lives of the Master Soul

The mission of Amilius, however, could not be completed in just one appearance on the earth. It was necessary that he, having taken on the earth's evolution, pass through all phases of human experience and evolve to perfection. He would do this by living many successive lives. Since he was the first in the spiritual realms to perfectly evolve into the companion of God, he would be the first soul in the earthly realms to perfect human life and bring the powers of God from the unseen into the *seen*. Amilius's role, according to the Cayce readings, spanned the eons of time that humanity has lived on the earth. As Adam, he allowed himself to fall under the subjugation of earthly appetites and temptations. Many would ask, "If he was the leader, the way-shower for the rest of humanity, why did he give in to temptation and have to be banished from the Garden of Eden?" In order for Adam to be the leader, he had to experience all the temptations and weaknesses of the souls who had gone astray. It was a purposeful experience.

Cayce said that Adam *allowed himself* to be led in the ways of selfishness. It was the only way that he, knowing full well the consequences of his vision dimming, could comprehend the experience of the fallen souls. Cayce detailed the many reincarnations of Amilius and gave an astonishing history of his appearances in the earth:

"Then realize that [Adam] is the same entity as mentioned who as Joshua was the mouthpiece of Moses, who gave the law, and was the same soul-entity who was born in Bethlehem [Jesus], the same soul-entity who in those periods of the strength and yet the weakness of Jacob in his love for Rachel was their firstborn Joseph. This is the same entity, and this entity was that one who had manifested to father Abraham as the prince, as [Melchizedek] the priest of Salem, without father and without mother, without days or years, but a living human being in flesh made manifest in the earth from the desire of Father-God to prepare an escape for man ... and this was also the entity Adam. And this was the spirit of light."[79]

It is a difficult concept for many to accept that the man we historically know as the master soul, Jesus, began in the beginning as Adam. Yet, Cayce again and again emphasized that life is a continuous experience; that life is an evolving process of God actualizing Himself through us. The great design of perfection takes many millennia to complete. Exactly what is this great design? It is summed up in the above quote: a manifestation "in the earth from the desire of Father-God to prepare an escape for man ... " As we would long for a child who is lost or missing or for a relative we were close to who disappears, this is an inkling of the longing God feels for the souls who do not consciously remember Him.

One embodiment on earth is not enough for us to fully realize ourselves as spiritual beings. What was begun by Amilius as Adam was completed only as recently as 2,000 years ago by Amilius as Jesus. The divine evolution was completed by one individual - one person who began the journey hundreds of thousands - if not millions - of years before. This is evidential of the grace of God who gives souls endless opportunities to work out their spiritual perfection in their own time. The miraculous reality of this idea is that each soul can and will eventually evolve to the perfection which Jesus attained. The following Cayce quotation sums up very well the purpose of each soul's mission in the material world:

"That it, the entity, may *know* itself to *be* itself, and part of the Whole; not the Whole but one *with* the Whole; and thus retaining its individuality, knowing itself to be itself yet one with the purpose of the First Cause [God] that willed it, the entity, into *being*, into the awareness, into the consciousness of itself. That is the purpose, that is the cause of being."[80]

In this we have the intimate story of the relationship between human beings and angels. We were once *conscious* of our communion with God and the angels. The whole of spiritual creation was in harmony with every soul. With the "cause of being," as stated in the reading above, it makes sense why there is the beckoning of the spiritual dimensions from the angel kingdoms - for we have been away and out of conscious awareness of the spiritual worlds for millennia.

The Angels and the Prophet Enoch

One of the instructional lives of Jesus was as the prophet Enoch. The experiences of this incarnation would serve him well in his lives to come. He would draw on his visions of seeing all the angels who cover every aspect of earth life. In *The Book of Enoch*, he is shown those who would govern all things in the material world. In his perfection as Jesus, He would command all elements of heaven and earth:

"After this I besought the angel of peace, who proceeded with me, to explain all that was concealed ... After this I beheld the secrets of heaven and of paradise, and of human action, as they weigh it there in balances. I saw the habitations of the elect, and the habitations of the holy. And there my eyes beheld all the sinners, who denied the Lord of glory ... There, too, my eyes beheld the secrets of the lightning and the thunder; and the secrets of the winds, how they are distributed as they blow over the earth ... " (Enoch 41:1-2)

Enoch describes the angels which ruled the movements of the moon and her sister planets in our solar system. He saw the angels who governed the light and the darkness. He witnessed the activities of the angel of wisdom and - as Dr. Rodonaia experienced - he saw Wisdom as a divine entity emanating myriad forms of enlightenment for the souls who learn to listen through the voice of intuition, imagination, and dreams. Enoch also saw the splendor of the stars, who are actually angels, and he learned that the virtues of each soul on earth was representative of the virtues of the angels. Their light shining upon earth in our universe is a reflection of the brilliance of the love of these angels. This mystical education was a preparation which would eventually lead to great miracles when the master soul, who was then Enoch, evolved into the soul who lived as Jesus.

"I beheld another splendor, and the stars of heaven. I observed that he [God] called them all by their respective names and they heard. In a righteous balance I saw that he weighted out with their light the amplitude of their places, and the day of their appearance, and their conversion. Splendor produced splendor; and their conversion was into the number of the angels, and of the faithful." (Enoch 43:1)

Enoch even glimpsed his future role as the Messiah, but did not comprehend that the vision was a prophecy about himself. The angel who was guiding him gently promised him that he would eventually understand:

"And I [Enoch] inquired of the angel who went with me, saying, 'What are these things, which in secret I behold?'

"He said, 'All these things which thou beholdest shall be for the dominion of the Messiah, that he may command, and be powerful upon the earth.'

"And that angel of peace answered me, saying, 'Wait but a short time, and thou shalt understand, and every secret thing shall be revealed to thee, which the Lord of spirits has decreed.'"

(Enoch 51:3-5)

As Jesus, this soul obviously understood a great deal of the secrets of the universe. His miracles in Palestine reflected them. When He was out at sea with the disciples, a great storm tossed the boat upon turbulent waves. Jesus commanded the elements of the storm, and they obeyed him:

"What manner of man is this, that even the wind and the sea obey him?" asked the disciples. (Mark 4:41)

The "manner of man" was one who had been taught that all things can be kept under subjection of the divine will if the mind is kept in perfect attunement with God. Enoch was initiated into the mysteries ("every secret thing shall be revealed to thee") and, in his perfection as Jesus, became the Master over all things in the material world.

The Bible indicates that humankind was created a little lower than the angels, yet when the souls who went astray return to the conscious awareness of their relationship with God, they will be the *rulers* of the kingdom of angels. Jesus was the first to fully complete the journey and return to conscious reunion with God. When Jesus commanded the storm to be still, He was actually commanding the angels who govern the earthly elements. His mystical education as Enoch was put into practical application as Jesus.

There is an interesting theory in the cabala, the Jewish mystical tradition, which indicates that the angel Metatron was formerly Enoch in the earth. In the Talmud, Metatron (which translates to "closest to the throne") is considered to be the link between the angelic world and the physical world and is charged with the sustenance of humankind. This aptly fits the role the Messiah would eventually play. If Enoch and Metatron are one, it is evidential that souls and angels change and evolve in the spiritual realms. Metatron did not remain with the rest of the angels; he went on to earth to evolve to *human* perfection in Christ. The readings indicate that between lives souls often act as guides and guardian angels to those still in the earth. This will be discussed more fully in a later chapter.

There are many clues in biblical literature which hint that Enoch was indeed one of the lives of Jesus. Many of Jesus' sayings in the New Testament are actually reflections of the writings of Enoch. For example, Enoch said, "The elect shall possess light, joy, and peace; and they shall inherit the earth." (Enoch 6:9) Jesus said, "Blessed are the meek: for they shall inherit the earth." (Matthew 5:5) Enoch laments over the fallen angels who choose to defy God: "Where will be the place of rest for those who have rejected the Lord of Spirits? It would have been better for them had they never been born." (Enoch 38:2) Likewise, Jesus is speaking of the great sin of the one who would betray Him: " ... woe unto that man by whom the Son of man is betrayed! it had been good for that man if he had not been born." (Matthew 26:24) Enoch depicts the souls who seek to follow spiritual law in the earth as eventually regaining their angelic status: "All the righteous shall become as angels in heaven." (Enoch 50:4) Jesus echoes the same concept in Matthew 22:30: "For in the resurrection they ... are as the angels of God in heaven." Also Enoch ascended up to heaven, just as Jesus did.

Throughout *The Book of Enoch* there is a reference to Enoch being the "Son of man." Jesus assumed this title in His final incarnation. "Son of man" actually is a literal truth in both the cases of Enoch and Jesus. Enoch was the seventh generation from Adam, who has been called the first man. In Jesus, His ancestry was from the house of David on *both* sides of his family - Joseph and Mary were each of this house which had a direct lineage to the generations of Adam. "Son of man" is a literal term in both instances.

Melchizedek - The Prince of Peace

According to the Cayce readings, another incarnation of the soul of Amilius was the biblical "prince of peace," Melchizedek. After the life of Enoch, Amilius returned to earth as Melchizedek in a unique way. Enoch had ascended at the end of his earthly life, and Melchizedek reappeared upon the earth but was not born of woman. He was an incorporeal being, yet he interacted with humankind. Through Melchizedek's unique spiritual manifestation, the earthly souls comprehended him as one sent by God. He was able to introduce a priesthood through which a lineage was created of the highest possible spiritual principles. This insured that there would be a way for souls to remember their divine origin and make great strides in the journey to spiritual reawakening.

Melchizedek makes his debut appearance in the Book of Genesis and is called "the priest of the most high God." (14:18) The name "prince of peace" was given to him, and this was also ascribed to Jesus. A Cayce reading described the life and virtues of this "prince of peace":

" ... there may be drawn to self a parallel from the realm of spiritual enlightenment of that entity known as Melchizedek, a prince of peace, one seeking ever to be able to bless those in their judgments who have sought to become channels for a helpful influence without any seeking for material gain, or mental or material glory; but magnifying the virtues, minimizing the faults in the experiences of all ... "[81]

Even in the Old Testament, the prophet Isaiah foretold the coming of the Messiah and called Him the "prince of peace":

"For unto us a child is born, unto us a son is given ... and his name shall be called Wonderful, Counsellor, The Mighty God, The everlasting Father, The Prince of Peace." (9:6)

In the Book of Hebrews, Melchizedek is referred to as the "Son of God" as was Jesus: "Without father, without mother, without descent, having neither beginning of days, nor end of life; but made like unto the Son of God; abideth a priest continually." (7:3)

Melchizedek was continuing as a leader and way-shower for the souls, bringing forth great knowledge and mystical talents never before seen on earth. His role, since beginning the journey as Amilius, was still the same: fulfilling the promise to awaken divine knowledge in the souls of the earth. Even St. Paul offers a parallel which indicates that Melchizedek eventually became Christ:

"So also Christ glorified not himself to be made an high priest; but he that said unto him, Thou art my Son, today have I begotten thee. As he saith also in another place, Thou art a priest for ever after the order of Melchisedec." (Hebrews 5:5-6)

He had lived as an earthly man as Adam and yet still retained the cosmological ability to appear "Without father, without mother ... having neither beginning of days, nor end of life ... " as Melchizedek. He came specifically in this form by the desire of God. In his well-researched book, *Lives of the Master*, author Glenn Sanderfur details Melchizedek as a vital step toward the perfection of humanity, led by the same soul who would become Jesus:

"In view of ... the rich messianic tradition about him which we have found, Christians should in no way find it demeaning to link the soul of Melchizedek with that of Jesus. Certainly both individuals were important instruments of God, and each life marks an historic step in the spiritual evolution of humanity."[82]

In His final perfection, Jesus was born as one of us, a Brother who set aside His position of being Master of all, so that even the lowliest would know that God manifested as an ordinary human being. This is the great mystery which had been hidden for centuries - that Jesus, who became the Christ, *became* an ordinary person and lived and died as such. He had His divine origin in the highest realms of God's creation; yet He followed us to the depths of materiality to show us that even *death* cannot destroy that which is of God. Rather than mere worship, Jesus wanted people who heard Him to follow His example; for this was the pattern by which souls could reunite with God.

Amilius, the master soul who began this great plan as Adam, led many lives as a human being subsequent to his life as Melchizedek. As Adam, Enoch, and Melchizedek, he had appeared upon the earth without having gone through the cycles of birth and death. Adam did die at the end of his life, but he hadn't experienced physical birth. Having perfected the ability to come and go in the earth's sphere without coming under the birth and death cycle, the master soul was ready to be born and die like the rest of humanity. Each life of Amilius helped quicken the spiritual belief systems among the people in different regions throughout the world. Each life built onto the next, coming nearer and nearer to a perfect manifestation of God in the earth. All along the way, he helped souls remember their divinity, taught them to meditate and attune to the Infinite.

In 1932 a reading was given on the lives of the master soul, and the following question and answer is particularly relevant as we look at spiritual evolution:

"What part did Jesus play in any of His reincarnations in the development of the basic teachings of the following religions and philosophies? ... Buddhism ... Mohammedanism, Confucianism, Shintoism, Brahmanism, Platoism, Judaism."

The sleeping Cayce answered, "As has been indicated, the entity - as an entity - influenced either directly or indirectly all those forms of philosophy or religious thought that taught God was one ... Whether in Buddhism, Mohammedanism, Confucianism, Platoism, or what - these have been added to much from that as was given by Jesus in His walk in Galilee and Judea. In all of these, then, there is that same impelling spirit ... there *is only* one [God] ... "[83]

The many lives of Jesus prior to His incarnation 2,000 years ago is a study in spiritual evolution which is not peculiar to one soul, but is very applicable to ourselves. *We* are the ones who are now on the road to this perfection, to the dawn in consciousness where we will be able to experience the Christ Consciousness with our own minds. Throughout the ages the promise from the beginning never was abandoned: Amilius was given the commandment to lead all souls back to their oneness with God. Through many lives and experiences, it eventually became a reality in Jesus.

Angels in the Old Testament

"The period from Adam to Noah represents the physical age," Cayce said in one of his Bible classes. "The period from Noah to Jesus represents the mental age, and the period from Jesus on represents the spiritual age."[84] The Old Testament is, therefore, the record of the physical and mental evolution of humanity, its passage through a myriad of spiritual experiences ever journeying onward to the fulfillment of the divine promise. There is a great amount of evidence in the Bible that the angels have remained ever vigilant in helping the souls on earth, as was promised by God when Amilius began his quest. There are many references to angel activities in the Old Testament; angels always acting in the capacity of messengers of divine knowledge and intervention.

It is confusing to many people that, in the Book of Genesis, God, through an angel, would announce the birth of a son to Abraham and Sarah in the latter years of their lives and then command that Abraham sacrifice this same son upon an altar to test his faith:

"Take now thy son, thine only son Isaac, whom thou lovest, and get thee into the land of Moriah; and offer him there for a burnt offering upon one of the mountains which I will tell thee of." (22:2) Abraham sets out to do what he is told, but at the last moment before he kills Isaac upon the altar, an angel commands him not to do it, that this was only a test. The waking Cayce shed some light upon these peculiar events:

"The offering of Isaac is a shadow of God's offering of His Son to humankind," Cayce explained. "Isaac was saved, because God stayed the hand of Abraham and furnished a lamb instead, which is the future of the Christ being offered for the sins of the world. For, when God gave His Son as an offering, the opportunity was in the hand of man to stay that offering - but man did not. Through relying wholly upon the promise and putting His *whole* trust in the Father, the Son was able to overcome death."[85] Edgar Cayce was frequently able to see the connections between the Old and New Testaments. He often observed that what happens in the early portions of the Bible are emblems of what is to come in the New Testament, as the above example shows.

There are further descriptions of angelic encounters in the Book of Genesis. In the latter portion, Lot prepared a feast for a group of angels and pleaded with God to save the corrupt city of Sodom. His plea was to no avail:

"And when the morning arose, then the angels hastened Lot, saying, Arise, take thy wife, and thy two daughters, which are here; lest thou be consumed in the iniquity of the city ... Escape for thy life; look not behind thee, neither stay thou in all the plain; escape to the mountain, lest thou be consumed." (19:15, 17) The Cayce readings say that one of the angels whom Lot entertained was actually a manifestation of the Christ spirit sent by God to help.

In our time, the warnings of the angels speak to us through our intuition and dreams. At times the messages come as a still, small voice which warns us to avoid a certain situation or circumstance. Many people will attest that when they defy that inner voice, there are great consequences to be paid. In the days of Lot and Abraham, the warnings and admonitions of the angels had to be physical manifestations because they had not sufficiently developed spiritually to hear the inner voice. Now that we are in the height of our spiritual evolution, we are capable of listening to the voice within and heeding the warnings. The voices of the angelic messengers still speak to all of us, but it is a matter of how keen our intuition is and how readily we listen to that inner voice.

In the Book of Judges, the angels intervened when the Israelites had immersed themselves in corruption. They announced the birth of Samson, who was to be a deliverer of the righteous. This is a pattern which occurs throughout biblical history: Whenever there is great oppression or evil wrought in the affairs of humanity, a physical teacher, deliverer, or angel is sent to help. The reality of this divine intervention should be fundamental to our daily awareness. If we find ourselves in circumstances where we are beset by darkness and doubt, there is *always* an avenue for divine help - but it must be sought and asked for. The numerous accounts of angelic encounters in our time is evidence that we have a great deal of help in moments of trouble. The many encounters being reported in books and television and radio programs should be taken as signs that we are guided and protected. It is important to realize that the activities of the guiding angels are just as active now as in the days of the Old Testament. We are always in the presence of the Divine; it is only a matter of our recognizing that fact.

In I Kings, the prophet Elijah feels beset by unworthiness and asks God to take his life. He goes off into the wilderness to die, but is nourished and encouraged by an angel. (19:4-8) Elijah would become very important in future generations. According to the Cayce readings, he was the one who established the School of the Prophets, which would play a vital role in the coming of the Messiah. This was the beginning of the community of the Essenes.

It is well to remember that the Bible is the story of *all of us* in our journey through the earth experience. What the ancient prophets and people of the Bible experienced we will go through as well. It is a beneficial spiritual discipline to read the Bible and understand that those same guiding angels are near to us now as they were to the prophets and people of old. The Cayce readings frequently recommend reading the Bible as a *personal history* - for it is the story of each of us and our struggle to work through our material distractions and reunite with God.

Particularly in times of great crisis and so-called "hopeless" situations the angels are especially active with us. Miracles do happen. The angels' role as rescuers is evident in the Book of Daniel when, cast into a den of lions, he says, "My God hath sent his angel, and hath shut the lions' mouths, that they have not hurt me ... " (6:22) There is a tendency to believe that these experiences happened to the ancient prophets because they were "special" or "chosen" by God. Each of us has been chosen and is seen as special in the eyes of God. The Creative Forces do not discern between the prophet and the common person. Only humankind judges who is "higher" or "lower" than others; and it is only an illusion.

Further in the Book of Daniel is the first reference to the archangel Gabriel:

"And I heard a man's voice between the banks of Ulai, which called, and said, Gabriel, make this man to understand the vision. So he came near where I stood: and when he came, I was afraid ... but he said unto me, Understand, O son of man: for at the time of the end shall be the vision." (8:16-17)

As Enoch was given a vision of the future, so was Daniel. The vision was of the eventual perfection of the human condition through the earth and the coming of the Messiah:

" I saw in the night visions, and, behold, one like the Son of man came with the clouds of heaven ... and there was given him dominion, and glory, and a kingdom, that all people, nations, and languages, should serve him: his dominion is an everlasting dominion, which shall not pass away, and his kingdom that which shall not be destroyed." (7:13-14)

The reference to the kingdom was not indicating a physical *place*, but a state of consciousness. Jesus said that the kingdom of heaven is within us. The prophecy given by Gabriel also indicates that the message of Jesus would encompass *all* "people, nations, and languages," meaning that the perfection of Christ's manifestation in the earth encompassed all the world's spiritual hopes and desires, including the world's religions. Even though in the days of Daniel the perfection in Christ was thousands of years off as we count time, it was a reassurance to the generations to come that the promise had not been forgotten, that God was and is still mindful of the souls of the earth.

Daniel is also given comfort by Archangel Michael, who gave an angelic promise that is applicable to all of us: " ... O Daniel, a man greatly beloved, understand the words that I speak unto thee, and stand upright: for unto thee am I now sent ... Fear not, Daniel: for from the first day that thou didst set thine heart to understand ... thy words were heard, and I am come for thy words." (10:11-12) The key passage here is "set thine heart to understand." When we desire to comprehend the spiritual nature of our lives, the very thoughts go into the ethers as a message to the celestial hierarchies.

Remembering that the force of desire brought the worlds into being, we know that all things will be shown to us if we place ourselves in a state of receptivity through prayer, meditation, and a state of expectancy for these things in daily life. We are just as capable to have communion with God as the prophet Daniel. The problem lies in our feelings of unworthiness. Hugh Lynn Cayce once said in a lecture, "If you feel yourself out of the presence of God, make no mistake about who moved." Spiritual awareness is always nearer than our breath, but there is a tendency to disbelieve that we are worthy of such experiences. Another comment from Hugh Lynn comes to mind: that the state of our consciousness depends upon how much guidance will be received. If we feel unworthy to commune with God, then that very thought becomes a barrier. On the other hand, if we believe and desire to know the plan of our spiritual destiny, it will be given to us through the very desire to know.

The coming of the Messiah was foretold again and again in the Old Testament by the prophets. This advent represents not only the physical manifestation of the Christ, but the inner awakening which was promised from the beginning to each soul. Although humanity has collectively endured a multitude of experiences in consciousness, that promise for redemption has never altered. In the New Testament, we find a fulfilling of that promise given to Adam, and many more experiences with the angels. The angels had been readied from the beginning for the great redemption of humanity. The books of the New Testament are the story of the beginning of the perfection in which God became *perfectly human* as Jesus and where a human *became perfectly God-like.*

The Coming of Christ - The Promise Fulfilled

The Cayce readings tell the story of a peculiar group of people who were outcasts from traditional Judaism: the Essenes, whose name means "expectant ones." This sect believed in mystical communion with God, studied astrology, taught reincarnation, practiced psychic development, and held the promise that a divine manifestation of the Most High would come as a human being - the Messiah - in their time.

Respected theologian Richard H. Drummond, Ph.D., spent many years studying Cayce's readings in relation to the coming of Christ. In his book, *A Life of Jesus the Christ: From Cosmic Origins to the Second Coming,* he detailed the purpose of the Essenes:

"According to the Edgar Cayce readings the primary purpose of the spiritual activity of the Essenes was to raise up persons who would be fit channels for the birth of the Messiah. Their tradition was said to be in the direct line of spiritual descent from the school of prophets established by Elijah ... "[86]

For more than 300 years, the Essenes had been engaged in the preparation for the coming of the Messiah. The elders reared twelve girls at a time in the consecrated setting of a church or monastery. They were trained in all areas of physical, mental, and spiritual discipline. The hope of the Essenes was that God would choose one of the girls to be the mother of the Messiah. They took quite literally the Old Testament prophecies concerning the coming and followed closely the ordinances of Elijah. The Essenes had no evidence, however, that God would choose one of their own to be the mother of the Savior, but they believed and had faith that this was the way. An interesting aspect of this story, according to the Cayce readings, is that Mary's mother, Anne, claimed that she had immaculately conceived Mary. This was confirmed in other Cayce readings on the early Christian epoch, saying that not only had Jesus been immaculately conceived, but that He was born of an *immaculately conceived mother*. Anne's claim was not believed by the people in the Essene community, but they accepted Mary into the temple service because of her exquisite beauty and countenance. The readings indicated that the phenomenon of immaculate conception had occurred in the past. What had *not* ever occurred was that a daughter who was immaculately conceived would also conceive immaculately. Hence, the purity was borne through three generations of spiritual perfection, from Anne to Mary to Jesus. This triune succession seems to represent the crowning glory of perfection in body, mind, and spirit.

As the story unfolded in Cayce's readings, in the latter part of the 300 years during which the Essenes had been expecting the coming of the Messiah, Mary was chosen by Archangel Gabriel to be the Savior's mother. One morning, as the girls were going to the temple altar to pray at dawn, a bright light shone upon her and there was a great sound of thunder. She was led to the altar by Archangel Gabriel. This was the sign for which the Essenes had been looking. Mary was thirteen years old at the time of the annunciation. After three more years of further training, discipline, and consecration, she was found to be pregnant at age sixteen. At this same time, another of the girls who had been one of the twelve, Elizabeth, was also visited by the archangel Gabriel and told that her son, John the Baptist, would be the forerunner for the coming Messiah.

Finally, the fulfillment of the ancient promise was nearing. At the time of the birth of Jesus in Bethlehem, the very morning stars which had sung in the beginning at the advent of Adam in the earth again rejoiced at the fulfillment of this glorious mission. It was a full, beautiful circle. Just as there was great joy in the angel kingdoms at the beginning of Amilius' plan to resurrect the consciousness of humanity, there was the renewed joy in Palestine that God was being *physically born* into the earth in perfection. The angels from on high proclaimed the glory of this perfection.

Now, in our time, we are entering the third such fanfare of the angels. As they were the prompting forces who guided Adam and the early souls through the earth, the angels were again active when Jesus came 2,000 years ago. Now that we have reached the end of the second millennium since Jesus came, we are in a time where true spiritual understanding is dawning in people everywhere. The angelic kingdom in all its glory is making this known in its activities with individuals and groups.

The Cayce readings indicate that Jesus' advent 2,000 years ago was a time of great consternation, political upheavals, oppression, and strife in the earth, and yet - just as today - Christ comes as the hope of the world.

Throughout Jesus' lifetime, He was in constant communion with the Most High, with the angels and archangels and with all of the powers of heaven and earth that came under His will. All things had been experienced by the master soul - and now in His final phase of the cycle of birth and death He would overcome the cycle.

The final perfection was His overcoming of physical death in the earth. In the readings, Cayce introduced the idea that death was originally created as a blessing rather than a curse. Through the laws of birth and death, souls could incarnate into the earth, live and learn the spiritual lessons which would further them toward their eventual reunion with God, and then depart from earth at death to view every aspect of the life just lived and set about plans for the next incarnation. Prior to the death experience introduced through Adam, the souls who were trapped in monstrous bodies could not take leave of the material world unaided. There was no *end* to the circumstances created by those souls in that prehistoric period. Through Adam, however, the soul could work on its spiritual perfection in the earth in intervals and, at intervals, return to its true home. It is a logical conclusion that as death was introduced in the beginning through Adam, it was overcome in the perfection of Jesus.

For many centuries Christ has been viewed in the light that He is in an unattainable status. He has been depicted as a supernatural being which should be worshiped, but not as something which we can *become*. There is a hesitancy, even among the faithful, to see Jesus as a human being. All along, however, Jesus' primary teaching was that we would eventually be able to do many of the miracles He performed. He is a picture of our future, our spiritual potential realized on earth. This was a promise, a promise that each individual soul contains all the elements of God, the angels and archangels, the very powers of heaven. The powers of the universe could be unleashed through proper attunement; the angels could be commanded to do the biddings of the human soul. Jesus' promise was that the things He did were not merely a possibility, but an *eventuality*. His role as the Messiah was to show us our future. This was the divine mission which the Son of God originally began as Adam and perfected in Jesus.

The readings indicate that the entire universe changed when Jesus was resurrected. The whole vibratory pattern of creation was altered because the first man had finally overcome the world and returned to God. Jesus' status after the ascension was in the planes of consciousness higher than the angels. Why? The angels and archangels never left the presence of God. Jesus embodied the Prodigal Son - one who went his way and returned *willfully* to his father's house. His position, then, became as one who rules *with* God because He had fulfilled what was promised. There is a much larger truth embodied in a verse in the Gospel of John than has been previously realized: "And there are also many other things which Jesus did, the which, if they should be written every one, I suppose that even the world itself could not contain the books that should be written." (John 21:25) This indicates the *millennia* of experiences performed selflessly as Adam, Enoch, Melchizedek, and His many other lives and experiences on through to His perfection as Jesus.

But His role did not end with the resurrection and ascension. The Cayce readings explain that because Jesus overcame birth and death and resurrected the body, He can now, once again, appear in the three-dimensional world as He did 2,000 years ago. There are remarkable stories all across America of people who are not only experiencing Christ in dreams and meditation, but seeing Him in three-dimensional form.

In G. Scott Sparrow's book *I Am with You Always*, one is left with the conviction that the Christ is present in many people's lives today as He was 2,000 years ago. This is why this particular time in the earth's history is vitally important. The Second Coming represents God coming into the spiritual consciousness of the masses. This is an inner as well as an outer experience. People are not only experiencing the Christ Consciousness through dedicated spiritual disciplines, such as meditation and prayer, but are having experiences where the Man Jesus comes to them and performs healings.

In this sense, the so-called Second Coming is happening right now in our time. This is one of the major reasons the angels are active throughout the world at an accelerated rate. At the same time of Jesus' appearances in the twentieth century, the manifestations of His mother, Mary, are also occurring all over the world - Medjugorje, Lourdes, Fatima, Garabandal - and the message from both Jesus and Mary seems to be, " ... lo, I am with you always, even unto the end of the world." (Matthew 28:20) Now more than ever do we need that reassurance in these days of changes.

The Angelic Promise - From Adam to Jesus

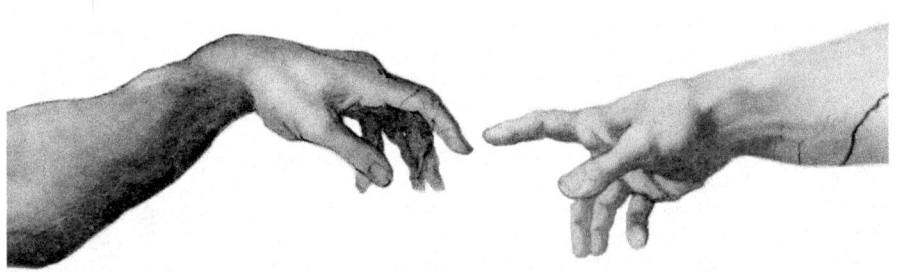

Chapter 8

The Book of Revelation and the Angels Within

"Blessed is he that readeth, and they that hear the words of this prophecy, and keep those things which are written therein: for the time is at hand." - The Revelation of St. John the Divine (1:3)

Angel Symbols and Angel Realities

THE Book of Revelation has been the subject of great discussion and debate for centuries because its message is shrouded in symbolism and mystery. Many fundamentalist religious sects hold to a literal interpretation of The Revelation - often predicting gloom, doom, and destruction in the final battle of "Armageddon" or the "end of the world." This chapter's exploration of angels in The Revelation, however, will look toward an *inner* interpretation, based on the insights that were revealed in the Cayce readings.

The Revelation was written by John, who was called the "beloved," the only apostle of Christ not killed during the persecution of the early Christians. John had been banished to the isle of Patmos, off the coast of Turkey. Cayce described the spiritual and psychic experience of John as The Revelation was given to him in the form of a vision:

"The beloved, then, was banished to the isle, and was in meditation, in prayer, *in communion with those saints who were in that position to see*, to comprehend the greater needs of those that would carry on."[87] (Author's italics) In the opening chapter of The Revelation, John describes this state of meditation as being "in the Spirit." (1:10) However he received it, The Revelation is a complex story of symbols, warnings, commands, and visions, which actually contain more references to angels than any other book in the Bible. In The Revelation, angels guard churches, books, and keys; they blow trumpets, pour vials, and stand in the sun. They preach the gospel and have power over fire. What do these angels represent and what can we learn from them?

J. Everett Irion, the scholar whose work is quoted in chapter 6, made a lifelong study of the Book of Revelation and Cayce's interpretation of it. He shed new light upon this mystical book in his own research, *Interpreting The Revelation with Edgar Cayce*, based on his more than thirty years of study. He interpreted the angels in Revelation along these lines: " ... all 'angels' are as the 'good' that goes out from each of us when we accept and work with others. As we meet each other in all our relationships, we are working with unseen forces. The spirit in which we do to one another becomes an angel or a devil according to our intent and purpose. An angel stands before the image we project to each other when we are seeking to harmonize relationships."[88]

We've already seen how angels ensoul principles, virtues, and ideals in the spiritual realm and how they do not waver from their purity in fulfilling those roles. To this, Irion's interpretation of The Revelation seems to add a personal, practical aspect; that is, that the ideals ensouled by angels operate *within* us as well. Whatever we create inside us, their energy, if it be pure, vibrates with the ensouling angel of that pure concept in spiritual realms. In doing so, angels, even from their lofty realms, act as connecting links between our behavior, thoughts, and actions, and God. Throughout The Revelation angels act as helpers to the soul to conquer the attitudes and emotions which form barriers to the conscious mind's communion with God. These angels are as real as separate beings, spirits, entities, in terms of how they operate within us.

The angels in Revelation are also reflections within the soul of the angelic hierarchy in the spiritual realms. Keeping in mind the idea which Cayce presented that all things in the earth are but shadows of what exists in the spiritual world, we may understand how these "reflections" of the angels within us can operate as our guides.

Edgar Cayce and the Book of Revelation

There were twenty-four readings given by Cayce which provide an interpretation of the Book of Revelation. The first mention of that biblical book by Cayce came during a reading for a young woman with mental problems: " ... for with pressure in the lumbar and sacral region ... corresponds to those forces as are spoken of, even in that of The Revelation. Be very good for the doctor here to read [The] Revelation and understand it ... in reference to this body!"[89] When he awoke from the reading, Cayce was intrigued by the reference to The Revelation as was his son Hugh Lynn. Because they were both avid Bible readers, the possibility of receiving an interpretation of The Revelation was quite exciting.

The remarkable dimension of these readings is the importance they place upon individual spiritual development and awakening. The Revelation, in this interpretation, is not the story of the end of the world, nor is it a story of mass destruction as so many believe. In contrast to this belief, the sleeping Cayce described the *inner meaning* of the symbols found within the book: "For the visions, the experiences, the names, the churches, the places, the dragons, the cities, all are but emblems of those forces that may war within the individual in its journey through the material [world] ... "[90] In this light, the Book of Revelation is the story of all the activities which distracted the soul from conscious awareness of God. Further, it reveals that the benefit of understanding it is "a new heaven and a new earth," (21:1) which translates, according to Cayce, to a new state of consciousness of the soul's oneness with God.

The opening verse in The Revelation indicates that these visions were *given* to John as a living record of Jesus' experiences and passages in the earth; His own mystical journey from Amilius in the beginning, to Adam, and to the attainment of the Christ as Jesus in the end:

"The Revelation of Jesus Christ, which God gave unto him [John], to shew unto his servants things which must shortly come to pass; and he sent and signified it by his angel unto his servant John ... " (Author's italics) (1:1)

"God had revealed to Jesus," Everett Irion said in his class, "by His learning the essences of the things which happened to Him in His journey through the earth plane, the true meanings hidden in the trials of humans in the earth."

Cayce often spoke of Jesus as being the pattern for humanity. All experiences He passed through toward His own spiritual awakening would be ours as well, if we but follow His pattern. The powers which Jesus had will eventually be ours when we are spiritually awakened. As we become aware that souls were created as co-creators with God, we will follow in His footsteps and *become* Christs ourselves.

Many people find The Revelation a frightening book, filled with visions of a world holocaust, catastrophe, and destruction. Barbara Marx Hubbard, author, mystic, and interpreter of the Book of Revelation, had some pertinent observations about John's vision in her book, *The Revelation: Our Crisis Is a Birth*. Through deep prayer and meditation, she received inspiring information about the future of humanity in relation to The Revelation and saw us each in various stages of becoming fully awakened spiritual beings like Christ. Of the frightening quality of The Revelation and how frequently people misunderstand the book, she writes:

"Imagine how your early ancestors would describe you if you visited them in their caves, arriving in your jets, flashing your images on portable television screens, talking to your colleagues on the moon. It would be almost indescribable. They would think of you as spirits, as gods to be feared and placated ... It would be hard for them to believe that they had the capacity to do as you do - and even

The Book of Revelation and the Angels Within

more ... "[91]

This is how John the Beloved saw his Master Jesus, the angels, and the drama of The Revelation which he envisioned. He was frightened because Jesus, as Christ, had reassumed His estate of being a co-creator with God. His countenance was *completely perfected* and in spirit bore little resemblance to the physical body He had occupied on earth. John was perceiving the spiritual future of the perfection of all souls in his vision, and indeed to us the images seem alien and frightening.

Because we are unaccustomed to the ideas in Revelation, we often latch onto the fearful and expect the worst: the coming of the so-called anti-Christ. If we turn our attention inward instead, we can understand how these are the very forces that rebel against the spiritual impulses within us.

Irion's approach to Revelation, he wrote, was "generally contrary to the widest acceptance of this book as a prophecy of the end of the world."[92] Rather than an end-of-the-world doomsday story, The Revelation is one of the most hopeful books of the Bible. But in order for it to be understood, one must turn his or her attention within and look at the impelling spirit of individual activity. Cayce gave a prophecy that those who really sought to understand The Revelation would become "as rivers of light, as fountains of knowledge, as mountains of strengths, as the pastures for the hungry, as the rest for the weary, as the strength for the weak."[93]

The essence of understanding The Revelation is found in practicing love in every aspect of life. It is understood when we continue to love ourselves - even when we fall short of our highest ideals and are faced with the "beastly" aspects of ourselves, the parts represented by the dragons and beasts in Revelation. The book actually becomes practical, then, when we are able to see the Christ in the condemned criminal as well as in the most godly of human beings.

"Then in thy study," the sleeping Cayce said, " ... Condemn no one. Love all. Do good. And ye may experience it all."[94]

Our present time has been called the "times of testing" in the Cayce readings. This is the homestretch prior to the new millennium set to begin in 1998. Each of us will be challenged in our own ways to learn to love, forgive, be patient, be kind, be *spiritual* in the material world. The readings are very firm in the idea that we cannot become Christlike alone. All we humans can do is attempt to manifest love. God enables and quickens us to become the embodiment of love. Often Cayce said that it is not in the end result that we succeed in our soul's mission, but in the *attempt*, in the trying to do good, that we are fulfilled.

In the attempting, we will be given more understanding until we reach the threshold of our true spiritual essence. All the mysteries of heaven and earth, according to the readings, are within us. These mysteries are not unattainable; they are as close to us as our will. And as we begin to search and apply the spiritual truths in our lives, then those realms of "heaven within us" will awaken and guide us intuitively, instinctively to a new way of being. This is the ultimate message of The Revelation - that the new heaven and new earth are waiting to be born *through* us. The truth is not "out there" somewhere, but is right where we sit in whatever circumstances we find ourselves.

" ... the whole of The Revelation is based on the unfolding of memory as experienced by the entity called Jesus and as recorded by John,"[95] Everett Irion wrote. The memory is the sum total of all of Jesus' experiences through His various earthly sojourns. Because Jesus embodied all of humanity's experiences in the earth, He is the Pattern and the Way. His experience is our experience. In essence, The Revelation is an intricate study of the spiritual, mental, and physical forces, laws, and experiences we all pass through in our journey toward the Christ Consciousness. We have known these things eons before we came to the earth. Yet once in the earth, we remember only that which we can apply in life. The whole experience of life *is* a revelation and, when lived in spiritual understanding, it is understood.

"Know first that the knowledge of God is a growing thing," Cayce said, "for ye grow in grace, in knowledge, in understanding *as* ye apply that ye *know* ... For this [The Revelation] to be practical, to be applicable in the experience of each soul, it must be an individual experience; and the varied experiences or activities of an entity in its relationship to the study of self are planned, builded, workable in the pattern as John has given in The Revelation ... "[96]

The Revelation represents a universal unfoldment of consciousness, but each person will experience it individually, in a way peculiar to his or her own soul's development. The prerequisite to fully understanding The Revelation of John is a desire to return to the conscious presence of God. For *through* experiencing The Revelation we are brought to the inner awareness of the divine Presence within. While the book is replete with emblems and symbols, it is important to remember that these represent actual living forces, beings, states of consciousness.

In our inner life, the angels mentioned in The Revelation are the guardians to carry us to higher, more spiritual states of being. *Each force represented in The Revelation is very real*. Through its study we will come face to face not only with our origin and destiny, but with our God. The path to understand The Revelation is indeed the way of the mystic. If the heart is set in the ideal of love, out of its study will come greater service, greater understanding, greater patience with our fellow human beings. John's mystical vision will unfold like a multifaceted flower before us, guiding us to the ultimate truth of our existence, the purpose of our being here in this time, our role for the coming age: to be conscious co-creators with God, completely aware of ourselves *and* God.

The key to Cayce's approach to understanding Revelation is becoming conscious of the spirit behind our activities and our thoughts. In this light, we can observe negative attitudes and emotions and see them take the form of dragons and demons, just as pictured in the Book of Revelation. On the other hand, the good we do - the purpose and spirit *behind* the act - shines like a beacon of light through the heavens, as the seven angels in Revelation are depicted. The issue at hand is how these *forces* (and that is really what attitudes and emotions are - forces) war within us, pull at us, take us apart on thoughts, feelings, and issues. But the pattern of harmony and inner balance already exists within the soul-body. Understanding The Revelation and its emblems will enable us to know what forces are warring as well as cooperating within us.

" ... well that you each here review within yourselves the experiences of The Revelation as related to your individual lives," Cayce advised in a reading. "In this manner may you each attune yourselves to the more comprehensive understanding ... "[97]

The readings stated that when the full understanding of The Revelation dawns within the consciousness of the initiate, he or she will not be able to put it into words. The whole of it must be lived to be truly understood:

"To me one thing is certain," Irion stated in class, "and that is that intellectual understanding is insufficient; for while this may give us verbal concepts, it cannot substitute for the understanding that can only come from living our experiences."

With this in mind, it is hoped that the ideas presented in this chapter will give the reader a glimpse of the meaning of the angels in Revelation and how they guide and direct and help in the eventual *lifting of the veil* of forgetfulness at the soul level. It might be said that Revelation is a book of remembrance of our true divine heritage. It is available, according to the readings, only by the gift the Master gave to humanity in His journey through endless experiences toward perfection. In this way, it is a spiritual roadmap to help guide us on our own individual journey toward that destined state of consciousness called heaven. Not as a *place* somewhere else, but as a state of being which is attainable here on earth.

The Angels of Acceptance
vs. the Angels of Rebellion

Part of the key to understanding this mystical book is the realization that we have given life to material experiences through our thoughts, feelings, attitudes, and desires, which take on a life of their own within us. What we dwell upon in thought becomes a spiritual reality through the power of desire. This was true in the beginning when souls found themselves with incredible co-creative powers and went to the realms of their own creation, becoming enamored in their individual worlds and then slaves to the very desires they created. This is re-creation at the level of the individual, of the ancient fall of the angels, the rebellion in heaven.

"For the visions, the experiences, the names, the churches, the places, the dragons, the cities [in The Revelation], all are but emblems of those forces that may war within the individual in its journey through the material ... "[98]

Within us, at the soul level, are the infinite realms which are replicas of the archangels of heaven. These are our highest spiritual aspirations and ideals that have been with us from the beginning - a spiritual reservoir which can open us to great enlightenment. But, we also have within us the representations of the fallen angels. These are the angels of the anti-Christ, the thoughts, desires, feelings which separate us from feeling at-one with God. There is the choice within each soul to experience life in the spirit of acceptance (which is a force, an angelic presence) or the spirit of rebellion (which is, as we've seen, the spirit of Satan). These active *beings* are at work within us every day, with every decision, every desire, every deed. The Angel of Acceptance and the Angel of Rebellion have their lesser "angels," which are the very actions of our thoughts upon spirit.

The Cayce readings have often said that each soul is "only meeting itself" in the earth realm of experience. We have been through so many experiences throughout our many lives in the earth that we are now only meeting what we have created for ourselves. These are reflected back to us by the people in our lives. Each experience in our lives, therefore, becomes an active lesson or truth that will return again and again to us until it is perfected in us.

"People don't realize the power of thought and desire," Irion said, during a twelve-week course he taught on the Book of Revelation in 1986. "They are calling upon the very creative forces which brought the worlds into being: thought and desire. These are *personified forces* within us which have a life that we have given them. In the unseen realms they have an identity, a personality."

Are these personified forces angels?

"Each thought and desire has a life essence which acts as a messenger to us," Irion replied. "In that sense, yes, these are angels within us."

All situations in life are given to us by the higher soul-mind which is attuned to its own guardian angel. Each experience is given to us as a lesson.

"The light and darkness we manifest in life," Irion said, "determines whose side we're on as far as the Angels of Acceptance or the Angels of Rebellion goes. My judgment passed upon another is merely my judgment of *my concepts* of another. In that I have judged my own self. Through situations, people, lifetimes, I am always meeting myself. The questions we need to be asking ourselves are these: In what spirit or by what guiding angel do I operate from in life? Dissension? Strife? Joy? Blaming others? Forbearance?

"The spirit in which I act will either release me or bind me," Irion explained, "just as there are angels who guide us to greater freedom or bind us closer to the earth-earthy consciousness."

If the spirit of acceptance is manifested in life - in whatever the circumstance - then we are freed. "And ye shall know the truth, and the truth shall make you free." (John 8:32) Irion taught in his classes that using positive affirmations to accept the circumstances of our lives will enable us to fully reawaken spiritually. For example:

> "There are no circumstances beyond my control. All I have is given me by my Higher Self because I am ready to meet or handle it. All is for my benefit and spiritual awakening. I accept all from the Angels of Love and Acceptance. I am, have been, and forever will be a co-creator with God. I release all that hinders me and accept the divine will of God."

Irion also mentioned that if we work with positive affirmations of acceptance, then we call into play the higher spiritual governing angels of God. We bring them into being in our consciousness, and they become living companions and guardians within us. Repeating spiritual words and phrases in an affirmation before meditation, during prayer, and in daily life is a powerful tool to "reprogram" the conscious mind to be more in attunement with the mind of the soul. These affirmations eventually become living principles in the soul and spirit, and any barriers to spiritual understanding will be broken down, and the mind of the soul will eventually become the conscious mind. Through Jesus' many lives, this was the pattern He set forth: that through making the individual will at-one with God's, God becomes the conscious motivating activity in the life of the individual. In this light, we *become* God, and God's power becomes us.

In understanding The Revelation, Irion teaches that it is important to understand that our reactions build actions. Each soul in the earth reacts to all it has created by itself, for itself. All experiences promote soul growth and awakening *if* the circumstance is lived in the spirit of acceptance. If it is not accepted in this spirit, the circumstance will return again and again, giving the soul endless opportunities to transform rebellion into spiritual growth. This is how we draw and grow from spiritual experiences. Our very thoughts and deeds return to us over and over until we learn the lessons.

"When a soul finally accepts its circumstances and lives them as a spiritual opportunity," Irion explained, "then it can move on through into a more sensitive perception of reality as that soul created it. There, at that point, The Revelation becomes a living reality and the soul is free indeed."

This is the key to living a spiritual life in the material world: understanding that we draw to us the influences that we need for our development. We draw the spirits (angels) of acceptance or rebellion through our state of mind, thoughts, and being.

"The experiences through which man passes," Cayce said, "as God gave in other periods, to become aware of his purpose for entrance into what we know as materiality [earth]. Then, the awareness of the *way* comes through the *thought* of man, the *faith* of man, the *desire* of man such as ever held by that One [Jesus the Christ] who became *righteousness itself*; passing through all the phases of man's desire in materiality."[99]

Again our very desire to come to a spiritual understanding in our lives goes out through the spiritual realms as a message to the divine intelligences, the angels; through them we are given the keys to unlocking the mysteries of the essence of life itself.

Angels and the Mystical Meaning of The Revelation

What follows is an examination, based on the Cayce readings, of Revelation's verses which are significant to our study of angels and the great spiritual consciousness which is being born in our time. Of particular interest are John's references to the "seven churches" in Asia. The topic is introduced in this way:

> "John to the seven churches which are in Asia: Grace be unto you, and peace, from him which is, and which was, and which is to come; and from the seven Spirits which are before his throne … " (1:4)

What did Asia and the seven churches signify? According to the readings, the reference to Asia in Revelation actually symbolizes the physical body. The seven spirits before the throne of God and the seven churches correspond to the seven spiritual centers within the soul-body (see Figure 3; also Figure 2 in chapter 7). There are physical glands within the body which correspond to these spiritual centers or chakras: the gonads, cells of Leydig or lyden, adrenals, thymus, thyroid, pineal, and pituitary. These ductless glands, which constitute the endocrine system, convey essential hormones to the physical body, but they are also the conduits through which spiritual energy flows into and through the body. These chakras are the same centers which were created in the beginning so that humans could journey through earth and yet maintain that all-important connection with the spiritual worlds.

Symbology of the Seven Spiritual Centers				
Spiritual Center	Endocrine Gland	Color	Element	Revelation Church
1	Gonads	Red	Earth	Ephesus
2	Cells of Leydig	Orange	Water	Smyrna
3	Adrenals	Yellow	Fire	Pergamos
4	Thymus	Green	Air	Thyatira
5	Thyroid	Blue	Ether	Sardis
6	Pineal	Indigo		Philadelphia
7	Pituitary	Violet		Laodicea

Figure 3
The seven spiritual centers and their related
symbols according to the Edgar Cayce readings

A study of the endocrine system is integral to the study of the Book of the Revelation," wrote Irion, "because the ductless glands play a great part in our awareness ... These glands are the contact points for communication between the soul or psyche to the body and conscious mind."[100] These chakras, which are referred to as churches throughout Revelation, contain all memories of the soul's experiences - millions of years of evolution are contained within them. The remarkable aspect of these chakras is that they actually correspond to spiritual sources within the body as well as *without* - in the unseen realms. During a reading, the question was posed to Cayce:

"What is meant by the seven lamps of fire burning before the throne, described as the seven spirits of God - Ch. 4:5?" Cayce responded, "Those influences or forces which in their activity in the natures of man are without, that stand ever before the throne of grace - or God, to become the messengers, the aiders, the destructions of hindrances ... "[101]

Not only do we have the inner circuitry to attune to the inner realms of the soul, but those angels, those guides who have been in communion with God since the beginning - when Amilius took form and became Adam - are *our intercessors*. They actively provide us the needed strength, grace, and wisdom to move toward greater spiritual awakening, toward the reunion with God. In this light, we have the guidance and guardianship of the angels without and within. The chakras are the centers of these spiritual activities. When spiritualized and awakened through meditation, the chakras become doorways to higher consciousness. Through them, we are able to experience the cosmic consciousness of Christ and a return to our awareness as co-creators with God.

The "throne" in Revelation is the culmination of all of our spiritual memories, even from the beginning of time. The throne refers to the memories held in the higher chakras - the pineal and pituitary. Cayce often stated that the body is the temple of the living God, the dwelling place of the individuation of God, the divine spark which makes us a soul. Through these centers we can experience the highest manifestation of God consciousness.

The Book of Revelation and the Angels Within

In a stunning example of how The Revelation can and will be experienced by all, Barbara Marx Hubbard was contemplating these words of the apostle Paul when her understanding of The Revelation began unfolding before her: "For as the body is one, and hath many members, and all the members of that one body, being many, are one body: so also is Christ." (I Corinthians 12:12)

During her mystical experience, Ms. Hubbard was prompted from within to write down what she had seen. This helps to verify the divine promise that all things will be revealed to those who seek to know their true relationship with God. In meditation, she was given an interpretation of the following verses from Revelation 1:5-6. The verse reads:

"And from Jesus Christ, who is the faithful witness, and the first begotten of the dead, and the prince of the kings of the earth. Unto him that loved us, and washed us from our sins in his own blood, And hath made us kings and priests unto God and his Father; to him be glory and dominion for ever and ever. Amen."

Ms. Hubbard believes that her interpretation was given to her from the Christ. This interpretation makes clear a promise to all: "I, who have made you kings and priests," she writes, "am now to make you co-creators. Women and men are no longer to separate for my sake, but to unite for my sake, whole being with whole being, so that you can become the second fruits of the dead - a generation that moves beyond degeneration to regeneration. I was the first begotten of the dead. You, dearly beloveds, are to be the next begotten of the dead."[102]

This promise of divine fulfillment is the reason for all angelic activity now infiltrating human consciousness. As the angels heralded the great coming of humanity - Adam in the beginning - and as the herald angels sang at the birth of the pattern of perfection in the Christ manifestation 2,000 years ago, they now stand as messengers for the Second Coming of Christ in us, in our consciousness. The biblical prophecies of the Second Coming take on an exciting and deeper meaning when contemplated in this light - that Christ is being born in consciousness *through* us. As Paul stated, we are each to become part of the great "body" of Christ, just as the many cells and atoms in our body make up "one" being.

"I am Alpha and Omega, the beginning and the ending, saith the Lord," reads Revelation 1:8, "which is, and which was, and which is to come, the Almighty."

This reference is particularly significant because it identifies Amilius - Alpha and Omega - who was the first son, Adam, who demonstrated the perfection as Jesus. " ... which is to come" refers to the remaining souls, the rest of us, who are on the road to becoming rejoined in God Consciousness.

The evolution of Jesus the Christ became a lifestream of consciousness which is a part of each soul who is in the earth. We are each patterned after this "beginning" and "ending," for we have journeyed with this master soul throughout the eons. This makes The Revelation very important to our spiritual awakening because it joins us as heirs with God and Christ - not separate or subservient - but equal to the Divine.

"The mystery of the seven stars which thou sawest in my right hand, and the seven golden candlesticks. The seven stars are the angels of the seven churches: and the seven candlesticks which thou sawest are the seven churches." (1:20)

Here again we have the symbolism which was presented in *The Book of Enoch*. Each star represents an angel which, in turn, represents a phase of consciousness within each of us. Seven is a mystical number of perfection and relates to the seven planets of the ancient world, the seven days of creation, the seven churches, the seven seals, the seven angels, the seven chakras. Symbolically, each of these lies within us, and through meditation each will be purified and be as guardian angels to our spiritual awakening. The Cayce readings say that the Lord's Prayer specifically relates to each of the seven centers within us. As we say this prayer aloud and visualize each corresponding spiritual center filled with light, we are actually quickening the process of our soul-mind toward awakening.

The Correlation of the Seven Churches and the Chakras

"Unto the angel of the church of Ephesus write; These things saith he that holdeth the seven stars in his right hand, who walketh in the midst of the seven golden candlesticks ... " (2:1)

The church of Ephesus represents the first spiritual center in the body; it is associated with the gonads. From this center springs the beginning of all creative activity. This center is the procreative and sexual energy within, but it can become a transformative light to the rest of the spiritual centers in the body. The energy begins as sexual, but can - by the power of the will - be transformed into spiritual energy. That this center "holdeth the seven stars" means that the power to be co-creators with God originates here, although its energy can be used strictly for self-gratification in the earth-earthy consciousness.

Evidence of the power of choice between earth and heaven at this level of consciousness can be found in verse 2:4, which reads: "Nevertheless I have somewhat against thee, because thou hast left thy first love." Our "first love" was the union of our consciousness with God, before the earth came into being. We left that love to pursue our own interests and creations and gradually fell away from this communion in consciousness with God. This "messenger" or angel of the church of Ephesus presents a choice for us to remain in the self-aware state of consciousness or to ascend to the higher realms and rechannel that energy in a fashion which is in harmony with God.

> "And unto the angel of the church in Smyrna write; These things saith the first and the last, which was dead, and is alive ... " (2:8)

This messenger within represents the perfect pattern from Adam to

Jesus - the Alpha and Omega; the beginning and the ending. This angel is represented by the second chakra, associated with the lyden center (the cells of Leydig in the testes and the hilus cells in the ovaries), which contain in consciousness the pattern for our perfect evolution. Through meditation, the body is "regenerated" from the raw earthy energy within it and transformed for spiritual awakening, a process which rises step by step, through the rest of the spiritual centers.

> "And to the angel of the church in Pergamos write; These things saith he which hath the sharp sword with two edges ... " (2:12)

This angel represents the third spiritual center, associated with the adrenal glands. The inner "fight or flight" activity related to this center is a double-edged sword. The first edge can cause great destruction and dissension within consciousness through warring with the inherent spiritual desire of the soul-body. However, the other edge of the "sword" is that flight can carry us to a state of spiritual at-one-ment with God. In the physiology of the body, the adrenal glands sit atop the kidneys and are ruled individually by the two hemispheres of the brain. There is a definite duality here - for the left brain controls the analytical abilities of our earth consciousness, and the right brain rules the intuitive, inspirational, and mystical experience. The angelic message at this center could be stated as: "Be at peace. Do not fight the spiritual impulse. Let yourself fly to the higher levels of God's awareness." Again, we are faced with material and spiritual choices at this center.

> "And unto the angel of the church in Thyatira write; These things saith the Son of God, who hath his eyes like unto a flame of fire, and his feet like fine brass; I know thy works, and charity, and service, and faith, and thy patience, and thy works; and the last to be more than the first." (2:18-19)

The Book of Revelation and the Angels Within

The divine messenger at this level represents the fourth chakra, near the heart, associated with the thymus. This spiritual center is the seat of love. The message represents a paradox in which we are constantly faced with the choice of manifesting either selfish or selfless love in our daily life. The spiritual attributes of this center are charity, service, faith, and patience. Here we have an example of the evolution from total self-immersion since the beginning of the "fall" to the ascent to higher consciousness where "the last [is] more than the first." In other words, in our perfection we will embody all that is at-one with God. The thymus center is the merging point of spiritual energy; it is of the earth, yet it is the midpoint between the three lower centers, representing earthly energies, and the three higher centers which are more heavenly oriented. This level of consciousness represents the bridge between heaven and earth, the four lower centers representing earth and the three higher representing heaven.

> "And unto the angel of the church in Sardis write; These things saith he that hath the seven Spirits of God, and the seven stars; I know thy works, that thou hast a name that thou livest, and art dead. Be watchful, and strengthen the things which remain ... " (3:1-2)

The angel of the church in Sardis represents the fifth spiritual center, associated with the thyroid. It is the seat of individual and divine will which separates us from the animals and lower creations: the will to choose. It is at this level that the soul can choose to defy God through the forces of will. Yet, when that will is made one with God, then the Christ mind is awakened; the individual will becomes the will of God.

The reference to death in the above verse is not negative, but refers to transformation or transition. At its perfection, our own individual will becomes transformed (dead) when we reunite with the Christ Consciousness. This parallels the death and resurrection of Jesus. His individual will passed through death, and then He was made higher than the angels because He had journeyed through all material experience and *willed* Himself to be at one with God. We eventually lose the individual will, yet become greater than we can imagine in perfection. The seven spirits of God and the seven stars represent the angelic assistants who help the soul in earth attain this divine state of will. This eventuality has the blessings of the Master Himself, as verse 3:5 indicates:

> "He that overcometh, the same shall be clothed in white raiment; and I will not blot out his name out of the book of life, but I will confess his name before my Father, and before his angels."

"He that overcometh" is directed to those who make their will one with God's. The reference to "white raiment" refers to the perfected aura. Each spiritual chakra vibrates to a given color. The gonads, red; lyden, orange; adrenals; yellow; thymus, green; thyroid, blue; pineal, indigo; pituitary, violet. (See Figure 3.) When the will is in perfect harmony with God, then these centers operate as *one consciousness*; there is harmony throughout the body, mind, and spirit. This harmony of all colors together is described by "white raiment."

> "And to the angel of the church in Philadelphia write; These things saith he that is holy, he that is true, he that hath the key of David, he that openeth, and no man shutteth; and shutteth, and no man openeth ... "(3:7)

The angel of the church in Philadelphia represents the sixth spiritual center, associated with the pineal gland. This chakra is the seat of all soul memory. Of this center, Everett Irion wrote: "He who remembers, knows, and no man can take away his memory. His memory cannot be shut off by another person. On the other hand *we* can shut a memory so far back into the darkness of forgetfulness that no man can get to it. In this vein memory seems to offer a valid understanding of what happens - as memory."[103]

All experiences we have passed through during our evolution in the earth are kept locked within the center of the pineal gland. In meditation, the energy rises through the seven spiritual centers and gradually awakens the memory of soul-mind through this chakra to universal love. At the level of the pineal, we remember ourselves as souls, companions, and co-creators with God.

Regarding the emblematic meaning of David, Charles Fillmore, founder of Unity church, wrote in his book *Metaphysical Bible Dictionary*, "David is often referred to as a type of Christ. His life was a forerunner of that of the more perfect man, Jesus Christ, who was of the house of David. David represents divine love individualized in human consciousness ... When David in his youth and purity daily communed with God, he closely reflected divine love ... "[104]

In this light, "the key of David" is the opening of the soul to universal love made manifest in the earth. When this universal love is awakened at the soul level through the pineal, then we are not swayed nor moved by material experience: "he that openeth, and no man shutteth." The angels in Revelation, therefore, are messengers of the divine memory of the soul's origin and also contain the pattern of the soul's destiny.

The following verse refers to this opening of the soul's memory and a fulfilling of the original plan of the soul's return in consciousness to the Creator:

> "Him that overcometh will I make a pillar in the temple of my God, and he shall go no more out: and I will write upon him the name of my God, and the name of the city of my God, which is new Jerusalem, which cometh down out of heaven from my God: and I will write upon him my new name." (3:12)

The "pillar in the temple of my God" refers to the awakened

spiritual awareness in the body (the temple). " ... he shall go no more out" means that once the soul awakens to the divine memory of its Source, then it will attain all knowledge from within - without having to search throughout the earth for the answers to the enigmas of life. In other words, the soul will no longer have to search outside of the self for meaning, purpose, and love. True understanding is given to the newly awakened soul. The new *understanding* is represented by the "new Jerusalem," a city (consciousness) of God. This awareness will ascend from "heaven" (the spiritual realms of the unconscious mind) into the "earth" (conscious mind).

> "And unto the angel of the church of the Laodiceans write; These things saith the Amen, the faithful and true witness, the beginning of the creation of God ... " (3:14)

The angel of this church is the seventh and highest spiritual center, associated with the pituitary gland. Everett Irion wrote: " ... in the body [the pituitary] is 'the beginning of the creation of God.' The pituitary acts as if it were the original Creative Force itself, for it does its job just as does the God Force which animates the body. It, in effect, gives life, *directs* the life force into action to the body in whatever the body-mind's choices are ... It is the seat in which the manifested ideas for [human] companionships are set in motion."[105]

This spiritual center does act as "the Creator" from birth to death: it holds within it the perfect pattern of the body, its shape, size, stature. The pituitary is the ruling gland in the physical body. Without it, there is no life. Hence we see why The Revelation refers to this as "the beginning of the creation of God."

When this center is opened in meditation, the person experiences "the silence," a vast reservoir of consciousness which is not merely an absence of sound, but a divine presence at peace and harmony. The attainment of the silence is the ideal of most meditators, for in this silence the whole body, mind, and spirit are in complete attunement with God. When the journeying soul attunes to this consciousness, there is a healing of every lower center in the body. The Cayce readings say that all lower levels of consciousness are stilled when the pituitary is awakened. They are subservient to the awakened God within.

The Four Beasts and the Four Angels

"And before the throne there was a sea of glass like unto crystal: and in the midst of the throne, and round about the throne, were four beasts full of eyes before and behind." (4:6)

The beasts are representations of the darker or shadow side of the four lower spiritual centers within. They are essential, however, in humanity's journey through the material world because they propagate the species, preserve themselves with the "fight or flight" mechanism, and keep the physical body alive through the sustenance of food. On the more negative side of their manifestations, the following question and answer came from the readings:

"What is meant by the four beasts?"

"As given, the four destructive influences that make the greater desire for the carnal forces, that rise as the beasts within self to destroy. Even as man, in his desire to make for companionship, brought those elements within self's own experience. These must be met. Even as the dragon represents the one [Satan] that separated self so far as to fight with, to destroy with, those that would make of themselves a kingdom of their own."[106]

Here we see the battleground upon which the higher spiritual influences war with the earthy or bestial influences within us. These beasts are representatives of the fall of the angels in the beginning, who came into the material world only to satisfy their own selfish desires. Just as the angels fell, so do the angels of our *ideals* fall within us, when we allow our highest spiritual aspirations to go unrealized. What is important, however, is the *journey*, the experience through all of these phases of consciousness. There is the darkness that the light may come and redeem it. Without the fallen angels, the fallen ideals, there is no redemption to save the soul. The darkness of the dragons and the beasts is the *unrealized spiritual potential*. When Light comes, it fully actualizes and transforms the beast into a higher, spiritual consciousness. This is emblematical during the process of meditation, when the energy begins in the lowest chakra - the animal nature - and gradually transcends to the highest God consciousness. It is the *same energy* - it is only heightened.

Cayce's group asked for further information on the beasts of Revelation: "Are we correct in interpreting the four beasts as the four fundamental physical natures (desires) of man which must be overcome? Give us more light on each of these."[107]

The sleeping Cayce responded affirmatively. He stated that they were symbols of the physical elements of earth, air, fire, and water. Each is outside of us, but each resides inside as well. The elements are helpful to us human beings, yet they also have their negative attributes.

The higher attributes of the beasts are represented in Revelation as the "angels standing on the four corners of the earth" in 7:1 of The Revelation. For every force or activity, there is the exact opposite: If there is light, there is darkness. The angels and the beast are actually *one*, but they become either helpful or destructive within us, depending upon how we apply them. Cayce shed some light upon these angels when he stated that they are only as from the "body-forces." He explained by saying they "are those four influences or forces in the natures of man from his source; as in environment, heredity as of the earth and as of the mental and spiritual."[108]

Here we see that these angels are representatives of the pure spiritual power within the soul. No matter how deeply enmeshed the soul is in the material world, these angels will retain the helpful capabilities to become the messengers to the soul in its spiritual evolution, as well as in physical evolution.

> "And another angel came and stood at the altar, having a golden censer; and there was given unto him much incense, that he should offer it with the prayers of all saints upon the golden altar which was before the throne." (8:3)

Remembering that they are actually divine messengers, angels in this verse represent the good we not only do in life, but the good we desire, think, and feel. Not only our highest spiritual aspirations, but each thought goes out from us to the unseen realms as a prayer to God. The Cayce readings say that the positive thoughts and desires become as angels that not only aid us, but help in the upliftment of the whole of creation. On the other hand, our negative thoughts and desires act as barriers and cause confusion and strife in our lives. Each thought is given *life* through the co-creative power of the mind.

The Cayce readings describe the "incense" in the above quote in this way: " ... that which has been kind, gentle, patient, merciful, long-suffering in self's experience during a day, rises before the throne of the mercy seat within self to that of an incense of satisfaction. Why? Hate, unkindness, harshness, all such become as base in thine own experience, and as usual one condemns self by saying, 'Why can't I do this or that?' And, 'What is the use?' Well - and the censer is broken!"[109]

The thoughts of self-condemnation, attitudes of low self-esteem, and self-criticism act as literal barriers between us and the angels who would aid us. Our own thoughts either make the way passable for divine intervention or block the way to where the soul finds itself in a state of self-alienation.

Attitudes as Angels

In Cayce's interpretation of The Revelation, we draw about us angels according to our thoughts, attitudes, and emotions. Upon our physical death, these angels become our guides to the dimensions we have created for ourselves. Every one of our thoughts and deeds, according to the readings, become guides, angels, intelligences which either move us to a higher realm of consciousness at death or hold us closer to the earth. What we hold to in spirit in the earth will ensoul the angel who guides us in the realms after death.

This issue was touched upon in a question to Cayce about the angels in Revelation:

"Do the seven angels described in Rev. 8-9 represent spiritual forces governing the various dimensional planes through which souls pass [at death] between incarnations on the earth?"

"This is a very good interpretation," Cayce replied. " ... as has been given, 'He hath given His angels charge concerning thee, lest at any time ye dash thy foot against a stone' ... If ye have loved self-glory, if ye have loved the honor of the people more than those thoughts of the mental and spiritual and moral welfare, what manner of angels will direct thee between thy interims?"[110]

Angels, in this interpretation, govern our activities according to what we do in our lives, in what spirit we act. The question remains for each of us: Are we listening to the angels? Are we listening to the spiritual call and *living* it? Or are we allowing circumstances to beset us to the point where life is chaotic and confusing? If the life is full of dissension, strife, chaos, hate, etc., then these will be as *living beings*, angels, for us when we leave this life. On the other hand, if the soul works to strive for happiness, peace, harmony, love, forgiveness, then these will be the ministering angels, the literal guides who carry us onward to higher realms of consciousness.

The New Heaven and the New Earth

The closing of the Book of Revelation is particularly inspiring, for it tells of a new state of consciousness, a new way of living which is to be a part of the spiritual evolution of all souls. John the Beloved writes of a vision in which there are no more struggles with the dragons, the beasts, the devil:

The Book of Revelation and the Angels Within

> "And I saw a *new* heaven and a *new* earth: for the first heaven and the first earth were passed away; and there was no more sea. And I John saw the holy city, new Jerusalem, coming down from God out of heaven, prepared as a bride adorned for her husband ... And God shall wipe away all tears from their eyes; and there shall be no more death, neither sorrow, nor crying, neither shall there be any more pain: for the former things are passed away." (21:1-2, 4)

The new heaven and new earth is the state of consciousness of the soul after its divine awakening. "Former things have passed away," Cayce said, "when there is beheld within self that the whole will of the Creator, the Father, the place of abode, the forces within and without, make for the new heaven, the new earth."[111] The entire journey through Revelation, the experiences with the dragons, the beasts, these all represent the struggle between the flesh and spirit; all that human beings pass through in the material world, constantly meeting and overcoming those things which are distractions to the soul. Even in the midst of the most terrible visions of the activities of the beasts in Revelation, there is always the presence of the angels, the guides, and the Christ. Cayce gave a glimpse of what the consciousness of humanity will be like after passing through these spiritual trials and tribulations:

> "Can the mind of man comprehend no desire to sin, no purpose but that the glory of the [Christ] may be manifested in his life? Is this not a new heaven, a new earth? ... For as the desires, the purposes, the aims are to bring about the whole change physically, so does it create in the experience of each soul a new vision, a new comprehension."[112]

From the Book of Genesis to the Book of Revelation, the Bible is the living record of humanity's evolvement toward this harmonious state of experience in which the soul is aware of its connection with

God. Cayce told many people that the Bible is the living record of *each person's experience;* not merely the people of old - but it is *our story* of the individual journey toward realizing God in the earth. This is an exciting time to be in the earth. It is not that we are simply supposed to gain this universal understanding of God and then leave this planet. Rather, we have all come together at this time to herald the "new heaven" and "new earth" spoken of in Revelation. Collectively, the more people who awaken a desire for this to be brought into being, there will then be a global transformation as has never before been experienced.

Everett Irion, in the conclusion of his book on The Revelation, summed up the exciting unfoldment which awaits each of us as we begin to experience our own version of the Revelation:

" ... we find the total evolutionary story of [humankind] in the earth culminating in [our] return to [our] Maker from the development of the physical in Genesis, the mental in Job, the spiritual in Jesus, all leading to the picture of [humanity] returning to and becoming one with the Creative Forces, or God ... "[113]

Whatever experiences we find ourselves moving through in our spiritual lives, we can rest assured that the doors of perception will open and reveal to us exactly what we need in order to move to the next step of spiritual awakening. The Revelation, as Cayce had said, is *individual.* Each person will experience the symbols, the angels, the beasts, in different ways. Through deep study, introspection, and meditation we can get a glimpse, however, of our own version of The Revelation. We can begin to glimpse that while there are angels outside of us who can aid us, there are also those angels within us, who can help to quicken and awaken our spiritual lives.

We find in the study of John the Beloved's vision that the ultimate responsibility for our state of being lies solely with us. Cayce said that there is no hereditary or environmental power that surpasses the will of the soul. Regardless of our circumstances, weaknesses, etc., there lies within us the very answers to all universal questions. The Revelation is in many ways the alpha and omega - it is the beginning of our spiritual birth in consciousness in the earth, and it represents the end of the long journey for the soul, with the help of the angels, to find its relationship to the Creator.

Chapter 9

Our Beloved Guardian Angels

" ... always the face of the guide or guard to each soul in its walks in the earth has its angel, its gnome, its face before the Throne of that which is the First Cause, the Creative Influence, God. And these are always ready to guide, to guard, if the soul will but put itself in the position in material things to be guided by spiritual truths."
- Edgar Cayce reading 531-2

Guardian Angels in the Arts

TERRY Lynn Taylor, author of several books on angels, interviewed rock musician-singer Carlos Santana in her book *Creating with the Angels*.[114] He believes that guardian angels have been influential in the artistic expression of his music. In Taylor's book, Carlos said that a turning point came in his life due to three people whose work had inspired him.

"In 1967 and 1968," Carlos explained, "Mahalia Jackson, Martin Luther King, Jr., and John Coltrane said, 'Who are you? What are you doing and for whom are you going to do it?'"

Carlos told all three people that he was a child of God and a musician and that he would always play and dedicate his music to God. His musical life, which spans four decades, has inspired and uplifted hundreds of thousands of people. Along the way, he had several experiences which confirmed for him that he was being divinely led by angels in his life. However, one experience in particular made him realize that his angelic experiences were messages from God.

Carlos had been notified by his record company that Julio Iglesias wanted to record one of his songs, "Europa," on an album. Iglesias would only record the song if Carlos Santana agreed to play it on the record. Carlos declined, sensing a vast gap between his musical world and that of Iglesias's. He felt that Iglesias was part of the mainstream record business, a system to which he did not belong and in which he did not feel comfortable. "I am a street guy," Carlos said to Taylor in the interview. "I just don't get along with the system … I'm still a hippie … "

That evening at dinner after the telephone call, Carlos Santana told his mother about Iglesias's offer. She was silent about his decision not to do the song, but it was a disappointed silence. After dinner he was getting ready to play a set of tennis. As he threw the ball into the air to serve, it *disappeared*.

A voice spoke to Carlos and said, "Who gave you this song?" Although awestruck, Carlos responded immediately. "You did," he replied.

The voice asked, "Well, why don't you let me do what I want to with my song?" Santana said, "What do you want to do with your song?" The voice replied, "I want you to record the song with Julio, and all the money that you get from it, I want you to pledge it to the children of Tijuana. You don't need it."

Carlos Santana's life was changed that day. He set up and arranged to record the song with Julio Iglesias.

"To me, it is all a lesson in humility," Carlos said. "I have to be wise and follow the voice. It has gotten me this far."

Guardian angels are those beings which accompany the soul throughout its material life on earth. Ever since Amilius journeyed to the earth as Adam, there were always the surrounding angelic beings who had never been to the earth in a material body. They were the promised guardians God sent to be with all souls in the material world. The Cayce readings indicate that each person has at least one guardian angel, whose role is to provide inspiration, intuitive breakthroughs, and spiritual experience as "reminders" that there is a greater purpose to the earth life. They do not *interfere* per se in the choices a soul makes, but they do prompt and guide people of like minds to be together. According to Sophy Burnham, best-selling author of *A Book of Angels*, it is rare that someone will actually *see* his or her guardian angel physically.

Those who are graced with artistic abilities often are in tune with the angelic realms. Whether it is painting, music, dance, theater, sculpting, these creative abilities come from the realms of angels. This is especially true of music. Cayce had said that music in the material world is a reflection of what he called the "music of the spheres," a celestial realm of angelic choirs. These choirs sang on the eve of Jesus' birth in Bethlehem. When an artist sits at the canvas, or a songwriter composes music, or a sculptor begins work on a block of stone, each one is drawing from these creative realms of spirit. Cayce said that music is a bridge between the finite and the infinite, and often recommended music as an aid for deeper meditation.

Medieval art is filled with paintings of angels. Many artists during this period believed that their inspiration came from the realms of guardian angels. Renowned artist Raphael attributed his artistic ability to depict angels to his inner visions. One day, two Catholic cardinals were watching Raphael as he worked on his angel frescoes. One of the cardinals remarked: "Why do you paint your angels with such red faces?" Without turning from his work, Raphael replied, "Because they blush to see into what hands the church has fallen!"

It was during the medieval era that angels were portrayed with halos and harps. The use of harps seems to underscore an angelic connection to the "music of the spheres," as Cayce described in his readings. The halos were indicators of the glowing energy fields or auras which often surround an angelic presence. When people see a physical manifestation of an angel, as Cayce did as a young boy, it is often enveloped in a soft white light. Others who see angels believe that the light emanates from within them. Since angels do not have material bodies per se, their form is made of higher, vibrational patterns of light.

One can look at the angel illustrations of Gustav Doré (some of which are found in this book), the angel engravings of William Blake, as well as the works of Michelangelo and see that the artists were inspired by something which went beyond common imagination to something spiritual and sublime. William Blake, an artist, poet, and engraver in the 1700s, said that he had visions of angels throughout his life. He claimed that an angel taught him to paint at a very early age and that the angel portraits he engraved were visions from angelic beings. Blake also claimed that his writings were dictated to him by angels and by Jesus.

Michelangelo stated that he could "see" the angel trapped within the block of stone or marble and that it was his job to set it free. The difficulty in portraying angels in a form acceptable to non-artists was brought to light in a humorous incident during Michelangelo's life. The pope confronted Michelangelo while he was working on the Sistine Chapel ceiling. "Whoever saw an angel with sandals?" the pope criticized. Michelangelo answered back: "Whoever saw an angel with *feet*?" Regardless of wings, halos, and harps that appear in their artwork, we have the Renaissances artists to thank for those inspired and visionary paintings. When one gazes upon their works, it seems clear that they were in touch with their artistic guardian angels.

Edgar Cayce and the Guardian Angels

In chapter 1, the young "men" who helped Marie when her car's transmission failed along the interstate were of the ranks of the guardian angels. They have the power, according to the Cayce readings, to appear physically in human form and help. Sometimes the guardian angel can manifest as a burst of insight or a sudden inspiration or a deep, innate stirring of the soul. Cayce in a reading for his wife Gertrude mentioned that the guardian angels can come as "an odor, a scent, an emotion, a wave, a wind … "[115] Many times the angels' influence is not physical, but comes in the form of a voice or a sense of reassurance. The readings were very clear that each and every person on earth has at least one guardian angel.

Cayce gave an interesting reading for a young man who miraculously survived a close call where he was nearly killed on the battlefield in World War I. Although wounded, the man was physically helped off the battlefield by an angel. The man later asked about the meaning of this angelic encounter in a reading:

> "In the angel stooping on the field, in the walking through the garden with the shadow ... the entity was being guided, or guarded, or protected, that that as had been promised from the foundations of the world would be to each individual, 'If ye will be my people I will be thy God.' He that walketh in the light, and purposes in his heart to *do, be,* that which *the* Creative Forces would have one be, shall *not* be *left* alone! for ... His arm, His hand, will direct thy ways."[116]

This is an inspiring promise to each of us: if we believe in divine help, it certainly will be there for us in periods of trial. In the above quote, God's "arm" and "hand" are the angels who are our constant guardians through life.

"To be sure," the sleeping Cayce said, "there are those consciousnesses or awarenesses that have not participated in nor been a part of earth's *physical* consciousness; as the angels, the archangels, the masters to whom there has been attainment ... "[117] Even though these higher angels have never been to earth, they can still aid the developing soul in the earth. Cayce emphasized the power of prayer as a means by which we may be guided safely through life's difficulties by the angels.

There are angels, unlike those mentioned above, who were once incarnate in the earth. These souls, having passed on, guide from the spiritual realms. This was the case when Cayce's deceased mother acted as Edgar's guardian angel during an especially difficult period in his life. Although he was able to help thousands of people with his physical and spiritual readings, he had many personal losses and deeply disturbing events in his life. Like all people, Cayce was prone to periods of depression and worry over the everyday things in life. He was always close to his mother and, as she had acted in the capacity of a mentor to him in his young life, Edgar always looked to her for counsel. Because of this, he took her death particularly hard. Even though he had enough psychic experiences to reassure him that physical death was by no means the end of the soul, the *physical* passing of his mother was almost unbearable to him. He wrote many letters to his friends and acquaintances asking for prayers that this grieving period might pass quickly.

Several years after his mother's death, Cayce had reached a period of financial crisis. He had left his photography business and was attempting to give readings full-time. Giving readings was never a lucrative enterprise as most of the people who needed help from them had little money. Usually, Cayce was able to get by, but in the early 1930s he was in financial straits. During a period of prayer, his mother appeared to him just as clearly as if she were in the room physically. She smiled sweetly at him and materialized a silver dollar out of the air. Cayce caught the coin in amazement and looked at his mother.

"Let this be a sign to you that you'll never have to worry about money," she said. "You'll always be taken care of." From that point on, Cayce felt reassurance from the other side that he was taken care of no matter what happened.

A similar experience happened to close business associates of Cayce's, Morton and Adeline Blumenthal, who were studying mysticism and spiritualism. The Blumenthals received more readings from Cayce than any other seekers. He and his wife were both highly developed psychically and had some fascinating experiences with spirit communication. Adeline's mother had been deceased for several months when Adeline began having dreams of her mother who apparently was acting in the capacity as her guardian angel. Adeline dreamt of her mother warning about the health of her sister-in-law. She sought an interpretation from Cayce and the readings.

"[I dreamed my mother said,] 'Something is wrong with your sister's leg, or shoulder … She ought [to] see a doctor about it.'"

In trance, Cayce replied, " … as is seen, the mother, *through* the entity's *own* mind, is as the mother to all in that household. Warning, then, of conditions that may arise, and of conditions existent. Then, warn the sister as regarding same, see?"[118]

Adeline's dream proved accurate and the sister eventually was successfully treated for her ill health which Cayce called "auto-intoxication and poor eliminations." Adeline and Morton had a conscious psychic experience right after she had given birth to their son. In the hospital room the couple experienced a phenomenon of lights. Cayce confirmed that the mother was just as near to them in spirit as she was in the earth.

Adeline had beautifully reassuring dreams of her mother's continued existence after death. She asked Cayce the meaning of an inspiring dream she had after her mother's death:

"[I dreamed a voice said,] 'Your mother is alive and happy.'"

Cayce confirmed this: "Your mother is alive and happy … for there is no death, only the transition from the physical to the spiritual plane. Then, as the birth into the physical is given as the time of the new life, just so, then, in physical death is the birth into the spiritual."

Adeline was touched very deeply and quietly asked, "Then, does my mother see me and love me as ever?"

"Sees thee and loves thee as ever," Cayce replied.[119]

Adeline's mother was very helpful to her daughter as well as to Morton, warning of accidents. In one instance, Adeline dreamed that her mother warned her about an impending accident involving her aunt Helen.

"When is this accident in danger of happening ... ?" Adeline asked in a reading.

"Within the present moon's phase," Cayce replied.

"In what manner ?" Adeline asked.

" ... street car and automobile accident," Cayce said. "Be warned of riding in either through these phases - that is, until the waning of the moon."[120]

It is fascinating that our recently passed-on loved ones often act as guardian angels. As was the case with Adeline, the souls of the deceased often appear in dreams to give information. The readings said that when we dream of people who have died, we are indeed in contact with them - it is not symbolic. Gradually, however, the soul gravitates away from the earth realm and moves on to other activities. However, in Gertrude Cayce's past-life readings, she was told that she served as a guardian angel for Edgar Cayce during an incarnation he had in Palestine at the time of Christ. She never incarnated during that period, but acted as a guide until Edgar joined her again in the spiritual realm.

These beautiful experiences portrayed in the readings should serve as reassurances for all of us. We never really lose those whom we love; they are with us throughout our earthly lives either as guardian angels or as companions in the earth. This understanding came to Darrell Cook (in chapter 1) when he found the robin's nest upon his mother's gravestone. He was not psychically sensitive enough yet to perceive her through his dreams or visions, yet she was able to act through physical circumstances to provide a reassurance.

These experiences should not be viewed as something unusual or unattainable. The Cayce readings indicate that we are *supposed* to have these experiences in our lives. It is only a matter of spiritual awakening. In working with our dreams, meditation, and prayer, we, too, will have the experiences of Adeline Blumenthal in which we are in direct contact with the spiritual realms.

Our Beloved Guardian Angels

A very peculiar aspect of guardian angels was given in Cayce's readings. They can be people who are still in the earth, but act as assisting angels during the sleep state. The readings indicate that during sleep the soul is not in the body, but is active in the spiritual dimensions. Cayce also went so far as to say that the dream and sleep states are a shadow of the realms we experience upon physical death. In sleep, we return to our spiritual consciousness.

Hugh Lynn Cayce talked about a woman who felt lonely, isolated, and without purpose and who came to Edgar Cayce for a reading. When she arrived, she was at the brink of suicide. In the reading, the sleeping Cayce told the woman that during her sleeping periods, she was in the spiritual realms helping souls to the other side who had been killed on the battlefields during World War II. She was acting in the capacity of a guardian angel while still in the earth! The woman was amazed because she could recall no dream experiences in which she had played the role of a spiritual messenger. But as she learned to work with meditation, prayer, and her dreams, she became familiar with her greater or higher self.

Hugh Lynn Cayce was answering questions at a lecture on this very subject in the 1970s. "Are our guardian angels separate from us," one man asked, "as beings who have never been to earth, or are they people we have known before, or are they an extension of our unconscious mind?"

"Yes," Hugh Lynn replied to the man, "all that and *more!*" His view agreed with his father's that our guardian angels come from many different sources.

A Psychic Boy and His Guardian Angels

Long before the current popular interest in angels, a little boy who lived in England during the 1880s detailed his many psychic and angelic experiences in personal journals. They were later published in the book *The Boy Who Saw True*, with a commentary by Cyril Scott, a psychic investigator who compiled the journals in the early 1950s. The remarkable thing about *The Boy Who Saw True* is that it is written in a child's language about the nature of auras, angels, gnomes, and fairies and includes conversations with the dead.

The child was clairvoyant and could "see" into the spiritual realms much in the same way as Rudolf Steiner. Problems within the boy's family arose when he assumed that everyone could see auras as well as communicate with the dead, just as he could. He was in quite a dilemma because his mother would punish him when he talked about seeing spirits or auras. However, he was comforted during those times by his guardian angel (whom he could see) who promised that those in the spiritual realms would help "arrange" for him to have an understanding teacher. Eventually a tutor, Mr. Patmore, was sent to the boy. The tutor was awed because the ten-year-old boy was able to see things in his tutor's past, a talent which indicated that the boy was quite psychic. After he got over his astonishment, Mr. Patmore became very attached to the boy and explored the spiritual worlds by asking him questions. Fortunately, Patmore encouraged the boy to keep the journals which today serve as some of the most coherent psychic literature about the nature of life after death and the spiritual dimensions available today.

The boy was consciously able to see the spiritual worlds just as clearly as we see our physical world. He would speak the words of his guardian spirit, whom the boy called Elder Brother, and Mr. Patmore would transcribe what the boy relayed. Of particular interest is this Elder Brother and the boy's late grandfather, who both served as guardian angels for him. On July 20, 1886, he wrote:

> "I saw Grandpa today, and he told me they (the spirits) had got papa to find Mr. Patmore for my tutor, and that they were very pleased with the way I was getting on."[121]

The boy had extensive conversations with his dead grandfather, who explained that spirits can often bring together people of similar interests. They can manipulate circumstances which help people come to greater spiritual understanding. In this way, not only do the angels act as messengers, but they arrange circumstances which are beneficial. Perhaps from this concept we can look at our lives and marvel at those so-called "coincidental" meetings of people who become our lifelong friends and spiritual mentors. Actually, the people we meet are not coincidental at all, but are planned and arranged by our guardian angels in the spiritual realms.

The boy's experiences with his Elder Brother (the boy referred to him as E.B. in the book) are of particular interest to the study of guardian angels, because he was one of the guardian spirits who guided people from their sleep states. This is how E.B. explained himself to the boy:

> "As I gave you no reason to think otherwise, I expect you imagine I'm a dismembered spirit? But that's not exactly the case. To be explicit, I happen to be a so-called Anglo-Indian, and I am communicating with you while out of my body which is asleep, thousands of miles away from here. Our night is your day. If it were not, I shouldn't be able to come to you like this. I have learnt to do work on this plane in my *astral* body while my physical body is asleep. [The boy] has the same power, and I often meet him over here. But neither he nor I remember it when we return to our bodies in the morning. Perhaps this seems strange to you, yet it's quite simple. Without special training, the *astral* body does not impress the physical brain with the memory of its experiences."[122]

This explains why the lonely woman who came to Cayce did not recall being a guiding spirit to those recently departed from the battlefields. The readings are very clear that at the conscious level, we are only aware of our personality-self. The purpose of a given life is to be as aware in the soul or higher self as we are at the personality-self level of awareness. The role of the guardian angel is to stir the soul so that it will seek to awaken to the greater awareness which it possesses. The Cayce readings state that all realms of consciousness are open to human beings, but they must study and practice meditation to fully awaken. A specific method of meditation recommended in the Cayce readings which will enable the soul to be in contact with the angelic realms is provided later in this chapter.

The young clairvoyant discusses many fascinating spiritual truths in *The Boy Who Saw True*. The young boy communicated with several different spirits from the unseen realms and correlated some concepts given not only in the Cayce readings, but in Swedenborg and in *The Book of Enoch*. As a ten-year-old, he relayed the following information about angels from (what he called) "the scientific spirit" to his tutor:

> " ... each element [in the earth] has its denizens, and ... there are fire-spirits, and water-spirits, and air-spirits and so on, and ... the two latter species have a certain amount to do with weather conditions ... the sun is the physical body of a Great Spirit ... the planets, including our earth, ensoul the spiritual bodies of great Entities known as the Planetary Spirits ... the magnetic forces emanating from the Planetary Spirits ensoul those heavenly bodies."[123]

This spirit also gave information on how the guardian angels operate in the earthly lives of souls:

> "An idea exists in *our* world before it materializes in your world; and that is why we are able to foresee the trend of thought and activities on your earth with a certain measure of accuracy ... "[124]

This explains how at a moment's notice, people are miraculously saved from impending disaster by guardian angels.

Our Beloved Guardian Angels

For example, a young woman was driving on an unfamiliar two-lane road in the Midwest. It was a winding country road without any security lights. To her horror, she suddenly saw a car which had swerved into her lane and was coming straight for her. The driver was apparently drunk and came close enough to her so that she could see the physical characteristics of his face. She knew that a head-on collision was imminent and blinked her eyes for a mere second, preparing for the crash. There was no time to move off the narrow road. After that split second when she closed her eyes, she found herself out of harm's way, the man's car visible in her rear-view mirror. As she drove the rest of the way home, she knew it was nothing short of miraculous that she was still alive.

According to the passage from *The Boy Who Saw True*, the fact of the impending accident already existed in the unseen realms. Because time is different in those realms, the guardian angels were able to intervene and prevent the woman's accident.

The author of *The Boy Who Saw True* remained psychically gifted throughout his adult life and helped reassure many people after World War I that those sons who had been killed passed on into the spiritual realm. He was able to contact souls of the deceased and give a message to bereaved families which relieved them tremendously. He could see clairvoyantly, with the help of his guardian angels, all facets of a person's life. Yet in his adulthood, he wrote that he was perplexed that he could not foresee tragedy in his own life. From his diary:

> "It is getting pretty obvious that our marriage is a hopeless failure. I have never complained to the E.B. before, but when, after my meditation today he suddenly appeared, I am rather ashamed to say I let myself go a bit. Why hadn't he warned me that I wasn't the right person to make J. happy? I confess his answer made me feel a little sheepish. He said in effect: 'We Elder Brothers do not exist for the purpose of circumventing the karma of our pupils. Both you and your wife have certain karma

to work off together, and had I warned you, I would have been frustrating the designs of the Lords of Karma. This is of course never permitted ... ' "[125]

The Elder Brother went on to say that only after an initiate "graduates" to a higher spiritual evolvement is he or she able to foresee events of his or her own life. In this sense, our guardian angels can guide and direct us, but the choices are still ours, and we must meet what we have created for ourselves - from this life as well as from previous ones. Although the circumstances must be met and many are quite difficult, our angels are always there to help us through the trials. But more than just their assistance, our becoming aware of them can make life a joyful experience - especially when we expect to be guided and directed by our unseen angelic friends. Terry Lynn Taylor summed up the importance of guardian angels in our lives in the Introduction to *Creating with the Angels*:

"Angels act as messengers of God. They communicate with us through inspiration. When we fill our everyday lives with spiritual essence and ask the angels to join us, we create angel consciousness ... Angel consciousness helps us keep heavenly qualities alive right here on earth. We not only see the beauty around us; we *feel* it in our soul ... Angels, as messengers of heaven, help us make life a true and meaningful experience."[126]

Meditation - Doorway to Communion with God and the Angels

In many ways, the dramatic new experiences people are having with angels in their lives can serve as signs directing the rest of us to turn our attention inward, learn to listen to the still, small voice within, and harken to our own guides, the angels who have been with us since the beginning of time. Learning to listen to the Divine through the process of meditation can open the spiritual doorways to our own guardian angels.

Our Beloved Guardian Angels

Cayce outlined a simple technique for practicing meditation which is effective in awakening the soul's ability to commune with the angelic realms, open up psychic abilities, and - the most important aspect of meditation - enter a realm where we become aware of God as a personal and present Companion. The readings say that in prayer we speak to God, but in meditation we listen to God. The readings went so far as to say that in meditation, we meet God face to face. It has been known to the mystics throughout the centuries that turning attention inward opens up spiritual worlds never before realized at the conscious level. It is in the quiet place of meditation that God will send messengers to us.

A young man of twenty-three years came to Cayce to ask about meditation and the processes of attunement. In this reading, Cayce called the guiding angel whom the man might encounter in meditation "friend," "associate," and "brother":

"If the approach [to meditation] is through some associate, some friend, some brother that is acting in the capacity as a sign, as a guidepost along the way of life, then know that thou hast been guided to that way - and ye yourself must walk that road; and that ye may not walk alone - rather with His guiding hand will the way be shown, will the way be made plain in thine endeavors."[127]

What a comforting message! To know that the road is never traveled alone. Indeed, for many students of meditation, there is a prevalent sense of "companionship" which is awakened after some weeks or months of regular meditation. The companionship is with God and His messengers. It is not that they are drawn *to* us through meditation, but that we become aware of angels *because* of meditation. As has been stated throughout this book, the angels have always been with us. It is only our awareness that needs to catch up with the fact. Meditation is a key to becoming aware of angelic influence.

It is important to practice meditating at the same time every day. This trains the conscious mind to be still. At first, a period of silence of fifteen minutes is sufficient. Then, as the body and mind grow accustomed to meditation, lengthen the period to thirty minutes - then to an hour.

In order to prepare the body and mind for a period of meditation, it helps to read some inspirational material or passages from Scripture for a few minutes. Instrumental music and incense were also recommended in the readings to aid in attuning the mind to the period of spiritual silence.

Keeping your spine straight, sit in a chair with your feet flat on the floor or cross-legged in the lotus position. Close your eyes and open with a prayer, asking for divine guidance and protection. It is recommended in the Cayce readings to say a prayer of protection, so that any angel, influence, or guide you may encounter in meditation will only be from the highest spiritual realms. Cayce gave this piece of advice about a prayer of protection to the young man mentioned earlier:

" ... when meditating or seeking for the opening of self to the unseen sources ... never open self, my friend, without surrounding self with the spirit of the Christ, that ye may ever be guarded and guided by His forces!"[128] In this instance, "His forces" refers to the angels and archangels which make, as Cayce put it, intercession for the souls in the earth to God. Opening with a prayer of protection also helps emphasize the purpose and ideal for meditation: to attune the self with the higher spiritual realms of God. It is also appropriate to ask for guidance and direction from your guardian angel. Here is a paraphrased prayer based on the Cayce readings which will insure that only the highest spiritual sources will help attune and awaken the soul:

> As I open myself to the Unseen Forces which surround the throne of grace, mercy, and light, I surround myself with the pure white light of protection found in the thought of the Christ. Only Thy will be done in and through me.

Our Beloved Guardian Angels

The Christ is called by many names. As it was indicated in earlier chapters, the spirit of Christ is the embodiment of *God in activity* or the movement of God. Throughout the ages this same spirit was present in Buddhism, Confucianism, Christianity, Judaism, Islam, etc. Whatever name helps awaken the individual to the highest spiritual ideal sought through meditation is appropriate.

Repeating the Lord's Prayer also helps the attunement process and was recommended in the readings because each of the verses corresponds to one of the seven spiritual centers or chakras in the body. Visualizing the body being filled with light as this prayer is said aloud helps to center the body, mind, and spirit for meditation.

Then a series of simple head and neck exercises is recommended so that the spiritual energy which moves through the chakras will not be hindered. These exercises should be done slowly. Do each of them three times. With the eyes closed, drop the head forward to the chest and bring it back to an upright position (3x). Let the head fall back in the opposite direction and return it to an upright position (3x). Then turn the head to the right, as if looking over the right shoulder (3x). Do this in the opposite direction as well (3x). Then drop the head forward to the chest and circle the head in a complete circle to the right (3x), and then to the left (3x).

All throughout the preparatory process for meditation, continue to think, feel, and visualize that your entire body, mind, and spirit is completely attuned to the realms of spirit. Visualize your guardian angels surrounding and protecting you. The readings often said that we are always in the presence of God; it is only a matter of awakening to the fact that we are. Meditation is one way to become aware of the abiding Presence.

A series of breathing exercises was also recommended to open the seven spiritual centers in a safe way and manner: Close off the left nostril with your index finger, inhale through the right nostril, and exhale through the mouth. Do this three times. Then close off the right nostril and inhale through the left. Upon exhaling, close off the left nostril, exhale through the right. Do this three times. During the inhalations, visualize your whole body being filled with strength, wisdom, light, and peace. When exhaling, visualize letting go of all limitations, problems, and tensions - anything which hinders you from feeling the spiritual Presence surrounding you. After the breathing exercises, use a series of words or a phrase which will act as an affirmation, something your mind can focus upon when it begins to wander. It may be something as simple as this:

God is love ... love is God ... I am a child of God ... I am now in the presence of God ...

The Cayce readings contain numerous affirmations upon which to focus during meditation which will aid in the spiritual awakening. In Eastern philosophies, an affirmation is termed a *mantra*. After the affirmation is repeated two or three times, enter into the silence. Don't be frustrated if your mind wanders at first. It takes time before there will be silence in meditation. The early stages of working with meditation is training the conscious mind to be silent so that the soul-mind can enter in. Whenever your mind wanders, bring it back to the focus of the affirmation. If meditation is practiced every day at the same time each day, the mind will eventually quiet down.

The repeated words of the affirmation become a message to the soul-mind to provide illumination. The words will eventually become an experience which will lead to the Silence - this is more than the mere absence of sound or words. The Silence is a place in consciousness in which you feel completely in harmony with God and the entire universe. It is a place where the feeling of spiritual companionship of angels is intimately felt. Many people report a variety of experiences from this state.

Hugh Lynn Cayce taught thousands of people how to meditate based on his father's readings. He mentioned that it is not unusual during meditation to have mystical experiences, such as seeing guardian angels or even seeing Jesus. We should *expect* such experiences to happen, but it is important to acknowledge the messenger, or the Christ, or whoever appears, and consider the experience as a sign that you're on the right track. It is important not to be distracted by the experience, but to be grateful for it and return to the Silence. This place of Silence is where Jesus promised that all things would be brought to our remembrance, even from the foundations of the world. Meditation is an important way through which we can listen, watch, and wait for the Divine's message and presence. Through this we can know the direction God would have us go in our lives.

At the close of meditation it is important to send out the energy which has been raised through the spiritual centers in the body. The best way to send it out is in prayer. Prayer is particularly powerful after meditation, and this is a good opportunity to pray for loved ones and friends as well as those who are deceased. Also prayer for peace in the troubled regions of the world is very important. The Cayce readings emphasized that nations could be saved from destruction by a handful of people sincerely praying and meditating for peace - and *living* it! Our thoughts, feelings, attitudes, and prayers are heightened through meditation, and the Cayce readings say that these prayers can become positive forces to bring about miracles in the earth.

Betty Eadie had the privilege of seeing firsthand just how prayers are answered by angels. She witnessed this phenomenon during a near-death experience she detailed in her best-selling book, *Embraced by the Light*:

> " ... I saw the sphere of earth rotating in space. I saw many lights shooting up from the earth like beacons. Some ... charged into heaven like broad laser beams ... I was surprised as I was told that these beams of power were the prayers of people on earth. I saw angels rushing to answer the prayers. They were organized to give as much help as possible ... The angels knew

the people by name and watched over them closely."[129]

Prayers which are given after a period of meditation help not only those who are living, but those who are deceased. The Cayce readings said that many people who have passed on often listen for their loved ones to tell them it is all right to go on. These prayers, offered after meditation, will no doubt be as one of the light beams which Eadie described that will guide the departed soul onward toward the light.

The Intervention of Guardian Angels

In some instances guardian angels do intervene in humanity's affairs when things go awry, especially during important spiritual periods of growth in the earth. A biblical example of this, discussed earlier, occurred during the time of Jesus when Michael the Archangel came to warn Joseph that Herod was going to issue an edict to kill all children two years of age and under due to his fear that a new "king" had been born. Michael's warning led Mary, Joseph, and Jesus to the safety of Egypt, where they remained unharmed.

Author John E. Ronner detailed a fascinating account of angelic intervention in *Know Your Angels*. In the twentieth century, hosts of angels were reportedly seen during World War I in 1914 at a battle in Mons, Belgium. Reports of "warrior" angels began to circulate among civilians, the medical corps, and soldiers in the British, French, and German armies. Germany was fighting the British and French, who were retreating from Mons. The battle was going badly, the French and British were clearly not doing well at all. Yet they began to win when angels were seen on the battlefield. A report from a captured German soldier stated that his army had to retreat due to a large division of white-clothed soldiers armed with bows and arrows, with an officer leading on a large white horse. The German soldier was perplexed because the army's leader on the horse was an obviously easy target, yet the Germans fired upon him repeatedly to no avail.

In another story told at the same time period, an army of white-clad angels stood between the British and German soldiers. The horses of the German soldiers balked and would go no farther, stampeding in the other direction away from the angelic army. At that point the British successfully escaped from the Germans. Still other soldiers on all sides reported seeing the figures of Joan of Arc, Michael the Archangel, and St. George, the patron saint of England. John Ronner wrote about this miraculous happening:

> " ... a wounded lance corporal claimed that his soldiers watched in silent awe for a half-hour as three striking figures with faces hovered in the sky about them - one of the celestial trio, seeming to have outstretched wings ... a greatly upset captain approached the corporal asking if he or any of his soldiers had seen anything 'astonishing.' "[130]

This account of the angels of Mons found its way into the newspapers and an earlier book was written about the mysterious beings who aided France and Britain in the battle in Belgium: *On the Side of Angels* by Harold Begbie.

The idea of guardian angels on the battlefield is not new. As discussed earlier, the "angel of the Lord" (which was probably Michael the Archangel) often delivered those who were righteous and who were called for a high purpose. In the Second Book of Kings in the Old Testament, Hezekiah, the king of Judah, asked God to save his people from Sennacherib, the king of Assyria, who had wreaked havoc across the nations and seized Jerusalem, claiming it for his own. The Assyrian king mocked Hezekiah and the ancient traditions of Moses, as well as mocked God's powers and abilities to deliver His people. Sennacherib spoke harshly against Isaiah the prophet and the people of Judah and would not give up Jerusalem. Hezekiah prayed to God and not only was Jerusalem saved from the Assyrian king, but every soldier in the Assyrian army was killed by "the angel of the Lord":

> "And it came to pass that night, that the angel of the Lord

went out, and smote in the camp of the Assyrians an hundred fourscore and five thousand: and when they arose early in the morning, behold, they were all dead corpses." (II Kings 19:35)

Shortly after this massive slaughter, the Assyrian king was assassinated by his own people. In this biblical story, the armies of the Assyrian king far outweighed those of Hezekiah's people. Without considering the unseen forces of God, it appeared that the Assyrian troops could take Jerusalem without so much as a protest. However, *one angel* took care of the entire Assyrian army! Likewise, Germany was clearly overpowering the British and French at Mons and - inexplicable in the rational terms of battle - Germany lost. This is a pattern throughout the Bible in the Old and New Testaments - and in the twentieth century. There are always seemingly insurmountable odds of good versus evil, and yet somehow a miraculous way of escape is prepared for the faithful few.

Angels - The Messengers of Hope

There is a central message in these biblical stories of the protective guardian angels, and it is always a message of hope. Earlier chapters described the angels who nourished Elijah; the angels who visited Daniel with visions of what was to come on earth; Enoch the prophet, who was shown the great and terrible visions of the angels of God and the angels of Satan, as well as the coming of his own destiny as the Messiah.

The New Testament has stories in which angels appear in the darkest moments when it seems that all hope is gone. At Jesus' birth was one such time when it seemed the world was losing its spiritual foundation. Cayce described in a reading the events surrounding the birth of Jesus and conveyed that this was one such time in history when, at one of the world's lowest points, hope was born again:

" ... lower and lower man's concept of needs had fallen. Then - when hope seemed gone - the herald angels sang ... All were in awe as the brightness of His star appeared and shone as the music of the spheres brought that joyful choir, 'Peace on earth! Good will to men of good faith!' "[131]

The Essenes, who were described in chapter 7, made way for a most unusual event when they prepared for the coming of Christ. They believed that deliverance was not only *possible*, it was *probable*. Among their own was born Jesus, who became the Christ. With the Essenes, nothing physically tangible indicated that the Messiah would be born among them except the hope and expectancy of it. Indeed, "Essene" translates to "expectancy" or "expectant ones," as stated earlier. Their faith brought about a miraculous birth and events which fulfilled the ancient promise that God could be fully realized and actualized in the earth. Jesus was born amid the turmoil and strife of a world which had lost its faith and nearly lost its hope. At that darkest point there was Light, and in the midst of it, there were the choirs of angels who proclaimed that a new hope had been born, a spiritual renaissance had begun as never before in the earth.

Now 2,000 years later, we are being reminded again to remember where we came from, to remove the distractions of the material world from our spiritual sight, and to listen not to the outside world which is in a state of chaos, nor be blinded by a world of appearances. But we are being led to turn *inside of ourselves*, where there is a reservoir of spirit which goes beyond words; a silence that's filled with peace, harmony, light, and - above all - hope for the next step in this grand spiritual drama being played out upon the world's stage.

The world today is passing through another period of darkness, testing, and transition. Communism has fallen along with the Berlin Wall, yet so many countries continue with age-old wars of hatred and religious differences: Bosnia, Serbia, and Croatia engage themselves in devastating battles. Mass murder and genocide in Rwanda. Hate crimes flourish in the United States. These are dark times indeed. Yet the forces of darkness and the powers of evil only have dominion over what we give to them. To restate Cayce's definition of Christ and the anti-Christ:

> "The fruits of the spirit of the Christ are love, joy, obedience, long-suffering, brotherly love, kindness. *Against such there is no law*. The spirit of hate, the anti-Christ, is contention, strife, fault-finding ... Those are the anti-Christ, and *take possession of groups*, masses, and show themselves even in the lives of men."[132] (Author's italics)

In these days of transition, we can fall into the trap of the anti-Christ, Satan, if we lose hope or our faith in the Divine. By doing so, we open ourselves to the very powers and fallen angels which have been examined in this book, those beings which warred with Michael the Archangel in the beginning and continue to "take possession of groups ... " We can, *by choice,* harken to the voices which bespeak of hopelessness. As we have seen, Satan is an actual force. But his influence is only through the material world and that by choice. If there are a handful of people who have lost neither hope nor faith, regardless of what hell the world appears to have fallen into, then the angels of light can assist those who hope and pray and expect the better outcome; the angels can then do their work in bringing about greater awakening and peace on earth.

Angelic messages of hope are springing up everywhere and are appearing in the newspapers, on television, in national magazines, and through individuals such as those depicted in chapter 1 and elsewhere. As in the days of the Bible, people are still chosen to become messengers of hope, such as modern-day seers like Rudolf Steiner and Edgar Cayce, among others. In the midst of great world darkness, there are those light-bearers who encourage us to carry on, have faith, and take heart.

The angels' manifestation in our time challenge us to look deeper beyond a world in transition. When considering the activity of angels, what do these experiences mean for us personally? Do they inspire hope within us? Do they enable us to be an angel to someone else? Do we believe there *is* hope for the coming new world? Now is precisely the time to really sit down and take stock of this remarkable world we live in and the miraculous events occurring around us. It is time to step back from the distractions of the material world and meditate and drink in the reality that, spiritually, we are not alone - nor have we ever been. It is only an illusion that we are separate from the divine light, the love of God. The angels - the celestial, multifaceted voices of God - are proclaiming that we belong to their realm of unlimited spiritual potential. It is only a matter of our realizing, believing, and manifesting it in our world. Now it is time to reaffirm that we are a part of God's divine plan and realize the promise which has been passed throughout the ages to the souls who entered the material world, words which Christ gave 2,000 years ago that have always been true: *I am with you always, even unto the end of the world.* For we need that divine reassurance, the comfort, and the message that God is forever mindful of us, loves us, and wants to speak with us. All we have to do is be quiet. And listen … listen … listen …

About the Author

ROBERT J. Grant began writing while serving in the Navy and authored five books including *The Place We Call Home* and *The Magdalene Diaries* (both now back in print through Hart Warming Classics). He made numerous television, film, and radio appearances, including *Ancient Prophecies* and *Sightings*. Robert was part of the team that digitized the Edgar Cayce readings, emerging as a leading authority, historian, and spokesperson on many facets of the Edgar Cayce legacy.

Known for his lively, extemporaneous, and humorous lecture presentations, Robert was a well-known speaker, historian, and workshop presenter on many topics in the Edgar Cayce's readings. He shared the platform with numerous New York Times bestselling authors including Brian Weiss, MD, Raymond Moody, MD, Marianne Williamson, Charles Thomas Cayce, and George Ritchie. He also conducted workshops throughout the US and internationally.

He passed away in Indianapolis, Indiana in early 2018.

Publisher's Note

THANK you very much for reading our edition of this book. Two previous editions were published by A. R. E. Press and were popular books for the A. R. E.

Robert Grant was very proud of this book, but really wanted to republish it with higher quality images of Gustave Dore's images. It took a lot of searching, but I found high quality scans of the images. I also added some other flourishes, mostly from the Rijksmuseum. Hope you like what I did with your book, Rob!

A little shout out to my friend Dee Dee. I was very much hoping to share this book with her when it was completed. She was tested a great deal her final years, but she never lost her faith, humor, and positive outlook on life.

We very much hope you enjoyed this book. We respect your feedback, so we would appreciate it if you left a review for the book on it's Amazon page. Reviews very much help to get the book seen by others.

Please consider gifting copies of the book to those you feel may benefit from reading it.

Thank you again!

James M. Hart
Hart Warming Classics
www.HartWarmingClassics.com

Hart Warming Classics

Other books published by Hart Warming Classics:

* **The Place We Call Home: Exploring The Soul's Existence After Death** by Robert J. Grant, ISBN: 978-4909069146
* **The Place We Call Home: Exploring The Soul's Existence After Death (Kindle edition)** by Robert J. Grant, ASIN: B07P19C81K
* **The Magdalene Diaries, Illustrated Deluxe Edition** by Robert J. Grant, ISBN: 978-4909069061
* **The Magdalene Diaries, Illustrated Deluxe Edition (Large Print)** by Robert J. Grant, ISBN: 978-4909069085
* **Frankenstein (Illustrated and Annotated 1818 Edition)** by Mary Wollstonecraft Shelley, ISBN: 978-4909069054
* **Frankenstein (Large Print, Illustrated, and Annotated1818 Edition)** by Mary Wollstonecraft Shelley, ISBN: 978-4909069092
* **Treasure Island (With Over 140 Illustrations and Nearly 450 Annotations)** by Robert Louis Stevenson, ISBN: 978-4909069023
* **Treasure Island (Large Print With Over 140 Illustrations and Nearly 450 Annotations)** by Robert Louis Stevenson, ISBN: 978-4909069030

Bibliography

Anonymous. *The Boy Who Saw True*. Essex, England: The C. W. Daniel Company, Limited, 1953.

Begbie, Harold. *On the Side of Angels: A Reply to Arthur Machen*. London, England: Hodder and Stoughton, 1915.

Bro, Harmon Hartzell. *A Seer Out of Season - The Life of Edgar Cayce*. New York, N.Y.: New American Library, 1989.

Bucke, Richard Maurice. *Cosmic Consciousness*. New York, N.Y.: Causeway Books, 1974.

Burnham, Sophy. *A Book of Angels*. New York, N.Y.: Ballantine Books, 1990.

Carey, Kenneth X. *The Vision - A Personal Call to Create a New World*. New York, N.Y.: HarperCollins, 1992.

Cayce, Edgar. *Psychic Development*. Volume 8 of the Edgar Cayce Library Series. Virginia Beach, Va.: A.R.E. Press, 1978.

Cayce, Edgar. *The Revelation: A Commentary Based on a Study of Twenty-Four Psychic Discourses by Edgar Cayce*. Virginia Beach, Va.: A.R.E. Press, 1945, 1952, 1969.

Cayce, Edgar. *The Study Group Readings*. Volume 7 of the Edgar Cayce Library Series. Virginia Beach, Va.: A.R.E. Press, 1977.

Cayce, Hugh Lynn. *Venture Inward*. New York, N.Y.: Harper & Row, 1964.

Crim, Kenneth, editor. *The Perennial Dictionary of World Religions*. New York, N.Y.: Harper & Row, 1989.

Danielou, Jean. *The Angels and Their Mission*. Translated by David Heimann. Westminster, Md.: The Newman Press, 1957.

Davidson, Gustav. *A Dictionary of Angels - Including the Fallen Angels*. New York, N.Y.: The Free Press, 1967.

Drummond, Richard H. *A Life of Jesus the Christ - From Cosmic Origins to the Second Coming*. San Francisco, California: Harper & Row, 1989.

Drummond, Richard H. *Unto the Churches - Jesus Christ,*

Bibliography

Christianity, and the Edgar Cayce Readings. Virginia Beach, Va.: A.R.E. Press, 1978.

Eadie, Betty J. *Embraced by the Light.* Placerville, Calif.: Gold Leaf Press, 1992.

Fillmore, Charles. *Metaphysical Bible Dictionary.* Unity Village, Missouri: Unity School of Christianity, 1931.

Fullwood, Nancy. *The Flaming Sword.* New York, N.Y.: MaCoy Publishing, 1935.

Giovetti, Paolo. *Angels - The Role of Celestial Guardians and Beings of Light.* Translated by Toby McCormick. York Beach, Maine: Samuel Wieser, Inc., 1993.

Govinda, Lama. *Foundations of Tibetan Mysticism.* New York, N.Y.: Samuel Weiser, Inc., 1971.

Grant, Robert J. *Love and Roses from David: A Legacy of Living and Dying.* Virginia Beach, Va.: A.R.E. Press, 1994.

Howard, Jane M. *Commune with the Angels.* Virginia Beach, Va.: A.R.E. Press, 1992.

Hubbard, Barbara Marx. *The Revelation - Our Crisis Is a Birth.* Greenbrae, Calif.: The Foundation for Conscious Evolution, 1993.

Irion, J. Everett. *Interpreting The Revelation with Edgar Cayce.* Virginia Beach, Va.: A.R.E. Press, 1982.

Komroff, Manuel, ed. *The Apocrypha or Non-Canonical Books of the Bible - The King James Version.* New York, N.Y.: Tudor Publishing Co., 1937.

Laurence, Richard. *The Book of Enoch the Prophet.* London: Kegan, Paul, Trench & Co., 1883.

Lewis, C.S. *The Screwtape Letters.* New York, N.Y.: The Macmillan Company, 1948.

Martin, Malachi. *Hostage to the Devil: The Possession and Exorcism of Five Living Americans.* New York, N.Y.: Perennial Library, 1976.

Nelson, Kirk. *The Second Coming.* Virginia Beach, Va.: Wright Publishing Company, 1986.

Newhouse, Flower A. *Natives of Eternity.* Escondido, Calif.: The Christward Ministry, 1937, 1944, 1950, 1965.

Newhouse, Flower A. *Rediscovering the Angels.* Escondido, Calif.: The Christward Ministry, 1950, 1966.

Peck, M. Scott. *People of the Lie - The Hope for Healing Human Evil.*

New York, N.Y.: Simon & Schuster, 1983.
Prophet, Elizabeth Clare. *Forbidden Mysteries of Enoch: The Untold Story of Men and Angels*. Livingston, Mont.: Summit University Press, 1983.
Redfield, James. *The Celestine Prophecy - An Adventure*. New York, N.Y.: Warner Books, 1994.
Ritchie, George, M.D., with Elizabeth Sherrill. *Return from Tomorrow*. Tarrytown, N.Y.: Spire Books, 1978.
Ronner, John E. *Know Your Angels - The Angel Almanac with Biographies*. Murfreesboro, Tenn.: Mamre Press, 1993.
Schroff, Lois. *The Archangel Michael*. Herndon, Va.: New Light Books, 1990.
Smith, Robert C. *In the Presence of Angels*. Virginia Beach, Va.: A.R.E. Press, 1993.
Sparrow, G. Scott. *I Am with You Always*. New York, N.Y.: Bantam Books, 1995.
Steiner, Rudolf. *Michaelmas and the Soul-Forces of Man*. Spring Valley, N.Y.: Anthroposophic Press, 1946.
Sugrue, Thomas. *There Is a River - The Story of Edgar Cayce*. Virginia Beach, Va.: A.R.E. Press, 1970.
Swedenborg, Emanuel. *Earths in the Starry Heaven - Their Inhabitants, and the Spirits and Angels There - From Things Seen and Heard*. London, England: Swedenborg Society, Inc., 1860.
Swedenborg, Emanuel. *Heaven and Hell - From Things Seen and Heard*. New York, N.Y.: Swedenborg Foundation, Inc., 1852.
Taylor, Terry Lynn. *Creating with the Angels - An Angels-Guided Journey into Creativity*. Tiburon, Calif.: H.J. Kramer, Inc., 1993.
Taylor, Terry Lynn. *Guardians of Hope - The Angels' Guide to Personal Growth*. Tiburon, Calif.: H.J. Kramer, Inc., 1992.

Endnotes

1. Reading 440-4.
2. Dr. Rodonaia passed away October 12, 2004.
3. Time magazine, December 27, 1993, p. 56.
4. Reading 294-1.
5. Reading 254-52.
6. Reading 440-4.
7. Reading 262-1.
8. Reading 254-42.
9. Reading 262-28.
10. *Metaphysical Bible Dictionary*, Charles Fillmore, pp. 700-701.
11. Reading 585-1.
12. *Michaelmas and the Soul Forces of Man*, Rudolf Steiner, pp. 13-14.
13. Readings report, 254-42.
14. Reading 262-27.
15. Reading 262-30.
16. Readings report, 262-61; Edgar Cayce Bible Minutes, p. 49.
17. Reading 262-28.
18. Reading 262-29.
19. Ibid.
20. *The Flaming Sword*, Nancy Fullwood, pp. 23-24.
21. Reading 1561-19.
22. Reading 294-208.
23. *A Seer Out of Season*, Harmon Bro, Ph.D., p. 375.
24. Reading 2897-4.
25. Reading 262-28.
26. Reading 2533-7.
27. Reading 262-33.
28. Reading 262-56.
29. Reading 262-57.
30. *There Is a River*, Thomas Sugrue, p. 310.
31. Reading 254-83.
32. *A Life of Jesus the Christ - From Cosmic Origins to the Second Coming*, Richard Henry Drummond, p. 73.
33. *Mystical Theology and the Celestial Hierarchy*, Dionysius, quoted in *Dictionary of Angels* by Gustav Davidson, p. 52.
34. Reading 5749-3.
35. Readings report, 262-56.
36. Reading 262-71.
37. Ibid.
38. Ibid.
39. Reading 254-83.

40 Reading 254-71.
41 "The Halaliel Question," W.H. Church, *Venture Inward*, May/June 1992, pp. 33, 34.
42 Readings report, 262-56.
43 Reading 254-71.
44 Reading 3976-15.
45 Ibid.
46 Reading 262-97.
47 Reading 262-77.
48 Reading 262-128.
49 *Heaven and Hell*, Emanuel Swedenborg, pp. 145-146.
50 *Angels - The Role of Celestial Guardians and Beings of Light*, Paola Giovetti, pp. 103-104.
51 a minute body or cell in an organism
52 Ibid., p. 48.
53 *Rediscovering the Angels*, Flower Newhouse, p. 66.
54 Ibid.
55 Chaldea was a Semitic speaking country that existed in the southeastern corner of Mesopotamia from the 9th or 10th to 6th century B.C.
56 Allopathic medicine refers to modern, science-based medicine.
57 Reading 257-123.
58 Reading 281-16.
59 Reading 1159-1.
60 *Dictionary of Angels*, Gustav Davidson, p. 176. The book can be viewed online at archive.org.
61 *People of the Lie: The Hope for Healing Human Evil*, M. Scott Peck, M.D., p. 203.
62 *Know Your Angels*, John Ronner, p. 67.
63 Reading 262-89.
64 Reading 262-52.
65 Reading 5221-1.
66 *Venture Inward*, Hugh Lynn Cayce, p. 130.
67 Reading 1297-1.
68 *Return from Tomorrow*, George Ritchie, M.D., p. 115.
69 Ibid., p. 116.
70 Reading 262-119.
71 *C. S. Lewis on Bad Angels*," quoted in *Forbidden Mysteries of Enoch* by Elizabeth Clare Prophet, p. 333.
72 Reading 262-52.
73 *Know Your Angels*, John Ronner, p. 66.
74 Reading 1968-2.
75 *Know Your Angels*, John Ronner, p. 66.
76 *There Is a River*, Thomas Sugrue, p. 311.
77 Of or relating to the Trinity; consisting of three parts, members, or aspects
78 Readings report, 262-61; Edgar Cayce Bible Minutes, p. 2.
79 Reading 5023-2.

80 Reading 826-11.
81 Reading 2072-4.
82 *Lives of the Master*, Glenn Sanderfur, p. 91.
83 Reading 364-9.
84 Readings report, 262-61; Edgar Cayce Bible Minutes, p. 7.
85 Ibid., p.1.
86 *A Life of Jesus the Christ: From Cosmic Origins to the Second Coming*, Richard H. Drummond, Ph.D., p. 11.
87 Reading 281-16.
88 *Interpreting The Revelation with Edgar Cayce*, J. Everett Irion, p. 193.
89 Reading 2501-6.
90 Reading 281-16.
91 *The Revelation: Our Crisis Is a Birth*, Barbara Marx Hubbard, pp. 89-90.
92 *Interpreting The Revelation with Edgar Cayce*, J. Everett Irion, p. 3.
93 Reading 281-28.
94 Reading 281-30.
95 *Interpreting The Revelation with Edgar Cayce,* J. Everett Irion, p. x.
96 Reading 281-30.
97 Reading 281-37.
98 Reading 281-16.
99 Reading 262-119.
100 *Interpreting The Revelation with Edgar Cayce*, J. Everett Irion, p. 11.
101 Reading 281-29.
102 T*he Revelation: Our Crisis Is a Birth*, Barbara Marx Hubbard, p. 86.
103 *Interpreting The Revelation with Edgar Cayce*, J. Everett Irion, p. 119.
104 *Metaphysical Bible Dictionary*, Charles Fillmore, p. 166.
105 *Interpreting The Revelation with Edgar Cayce*, J. Everett Irion, p. 126.
106 Reading 281-16.
107 Reading 281-29.
108 Ibid.
109 Reading 281-30.
110 Ibid.
111 Reading 281-16.
112 Reading 281-37.
113 *Interpreting The Revelation with Edgar Cayce*, J. Everett Irion, p. 438.
114 *Creating with the Angels*, Terry Lynn Taylor, pp. 176-186.
115 Reading 538-58.
116 Reading 1909-3.
117 Reading 5755-2.
118 Reading 136-45.
119 Reading 136-33.
120 Reading 136-48.
121 *The Boy Who Saw True*, with commentary by Cyril Scott, p. 97.
122 Ibid., p. 144.
123 Ibid., p. 182.
124 Ibid., p. 184.

125 Ibid., p. 209.
126 *Creating with the Angels*, Terry Lynn Taylor, p. xiii.
127 Reading 440-8.
128 Ibid.
129 *Embraced by the Light*, Betty Eadie, pp. 103, 121.
130 *Know Your Angels*, John Ronner, p. 23.
131 Reading 5749-15.
132 Reading 281-16.

www.ingramcontent.com/pod-product-compliance
Lightning Source LLC
LaVergne TN
LVHW051827080426
835512LV00018B/2759